A Death In The Family

Stories Obituaries Tell

Donna McCart Sharkey

A Death In The Family: Stories Obituaries Tell

Donna McCart Sharkey

Demeter Press
PO Box 197
Coe Hill, Ontario
Canada
K0L 1P0
Tel: 289-383-0134
Email: info@demeterpress.org
Website: www.demeterpress.org

Demeter Press logo based on the sculpture "Demeter" by Maria-Luise Bodirsky www.keramik-atelier.bodirsky.de

Printed and Bound in Canada

Cover artwork: *Winter's Journey* by Linda Rosalie Fox, 1931–2021
Typesetting: Michelle Pirovich
Proof reading: Jena Woodhouse

Library and Archives Canada Cataloguing in Publication
Title: A death in the family: stories obits tell / by Donna McCart Sharkey.
Names: Sharkey, Donna, author.
Identifiers: Canadiana 20230560148 | ISBN 9781772584653 (softcover)
Subjects: LCSH: Obituaries. | LCSH: Biography—21st century. | LCSH: Death. | LCSH: Parental grief.
Classification: LCC CT121.S53 2023 | DDC 920—dc23

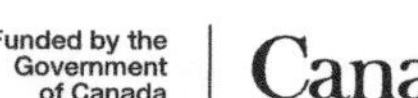

The publisher gratefully acknowledges the support of the Government of Canada

For Daisy, Tom Sr., Robert Henry, Florence, Tom, Irene,
Lyda, Georgie, Alessandra, and Brenda

And for Poppy, Kuzka, and Tidy

Obituaries:
Published notices, often with a short biography
or description of the deceased.

But really, are they only that?

NOTE: The obits and fragments of obits in this book
were taken from one newspaper. Some names were changed
and once in a while, age and date of birth are provided.

Acknowledgments

With many thanks to my brilliant publisher at Demeter Press, Andrea O'Reilly, who creatively recognized that women, family structures, relationships, culture, history, and norms may be well viewed through contemporary obituaries.

Much appreciation to my awesome editor, Anita Lahey, whose wise encouragement and support have been invaluable to this project. It has been a joy to work with her. And much appreciation also to Jesse O'Reilly-Conlin, my wonderful copy editor.

To my friends who are keen readers of obituaries and who share with me the delight in finding a curious obituary.

To all those whose obituaries and fragments of obituaries are included in this book.

With gratitude to Bobby, my sweet and winsome dog, by my side always.

And finally, much love to my daughter Alessandra, whose obituary, not included in this book, was nevertheless the most difficult for me to read.

Contents

Chapter 1

Obituaries and Me

Families look to remember their newly dead, to describe the person they were, who they loved, what they engaged in, what they liked and didn't. A time to fashion a family member's life, to highlight chosen aspects about them, correct misconceptions, step into their shoes, and put their best foot forward. They were the best. They earned the positives said about them. We knew them. We matter too. If it's me next, I too want a robust summary.

Each life considered in this book is an ordinary one, which is most of us: no one whose name lights up media tracks, but each holding its own special style, idiomatic, at times wondrous. Each life uncommon, a particular way of being here for a small or even large number of days.

Slanted with hope, he joins his father, she is reunited with her husband, predeceased by his son. Slanted with partiality, she fought long against that terrible disease. At nineteen, he died suddenly at home; no cause of death indicated. Died with assistance after an intolerable illness. Left her family after a life of struggle with her demons.

Slanted with love, our dad loved his dog, Gracie. Slanted with ideology, status, and qualities, our mum was an architect, our sister was kind to those less fortunate, our brother a proud employee of thirty-five years in a paint store or an appliance company.

Slanted, just as life slants towards earth. The concluding essay of a terminated life. The summing up.

Not all obits are completely truthful—the clichés, the gloss-overs: the best mother in the world, the most loving father, the most brilliant chess player, the person towards whom everyone gravitates. Yes, some people are placed on pedestals held by mythic status. But some families do count their deceased as scoundrels, ill-intentioned, or tightly wired. Illustrating shortcomings as well as laying out successes brings authenticity to obits. Some dare speak in ways that hint at a nagging character flaw, although certain words are never used—no one is ever mean, selfish, or stingy. These words blotted out, although braggard, upstart, and know-it-all provide clues. No one would deny that her temper was swift. He bragged about everything from A to Z.

Dying frequently occurs in cohorts. For three consecutive days several deceased people might be geologists, or firefighters, farmers, or nuns, ministers, or priests. There might be a week with a number of people over one hundred, or a grouping of people in their early forties, or several people in one day all sixty-four or fifty-one. Days with a clutch of golfers, or doctors, or teens. Three days when a cluster of people die by suicide. And over the winter holidays, obits sadder than usual appear.

There are days that would have you believe that almost everyone who has recently died had a hilarious sense of humour, wishing they could have told one more joke. But the leaving behind, her partner and best friend, four children, a sister, seven grandchildren. All named, partners bracketed. Left behind, to follow.

Exploring the world through obituaries takes us beyond biography and autobiography to social history and a gauge of society, of cultures, beliefs—of margins seeking boundaries. An anthropologist's playground.

Obits, a people's history of the world that is, a world that was, a world with ways vastly unfamiliar, a rendering of today's cultures, customs, and values. Quirky, tender, unusual, surprising, and suggesting to us the cosmic: where will you be after you die? what will you do? what is the meaning?

This form of personal narrative is often disparaged, the assumption being that an obit is merely platitudinous, bearing little resemblance to the person in life. Turning from this assumption and guided for ten years by compelling obituaries, I have found the endearing in obits, shining, as they do, a light on a person's life.

Some are master classes in comedy. They are hilarious. Read those ones and roar. Some offer examples of love for others, the world, themselves, of sadness swirling within grief. Some provide articulations of successes and failures—although fewer failures than successes.

Obituaries remind us of our fragility, of the limitations of time, of what matters.

These modest texts point to the importance of each life.

And ultimately, each obit holds a story.

It has been suggested to me that to read obituaries might be a weird activity. Full disclosure: I am a daily reader of newspaper obituaries, although they're actually death notices, but that's rarely corrected. Tiny hand-picked stories where so many people having accomplished much, or sort of, or not; having loved, perhaps, or not. These stories together contain such variety, each obit unique, forming a wild untamed garden.

I don't read all the obits. I skim past the clichéd, the proforma that cookie cut, mark only the skeleton of a life: birth and death dates, the list of deceased loved ones, leading with the parents gone before and sometimes siblings, then the left-behind ones wrapped in order of familial status and importance: loving partner of, doting mother of.

But I make note after note of those lives that stir my heart, those whom I might wish to have known, whom I miss not having met. So many people passing through in their own way, having lived through their own circumstances. The adding up, the realization that on no day is there no obituary. There is never a day without deaths. No break in dying.

Since she was eight, my friend Sue has read obituaries alongside Dear Abby. But I haven't always read the obits. For a long time, I skipped past their pages in the paper. Then my daughter, Alessandra, died suddenly one night, the middle of that night. When I reached for the screaming phone and heard, my heart pushed from its holding place, groaned with the pushing, my breath shoved my belly in and out, making the air hard for breathing. My lips quickly became parched, salted harsh from collapsed tears. My brain whirled with a head hurting rhythm to understand, figure it out, to make sense of it.

I was profoundly altered.

Four months after my daughter's death, I started to read obituaries. I needed to; I craved information about other young adults who had died. Each day I set out on a search to find answers, any similarity, to find somewhere another mother saturated in loss, to find I wasn't alone. I read obits each day, and the more I read them, the more my enthralment of how, every day, the notices pile up. At times I paused at an obit, someone who lived slanted, and I would never know more about them than what those six hundred words provided me.

But the thoughtfully expressed portrayals, these captivating mini-biographies, and at times autobiographies, invited me to keep them in a file just for them. Over close to a decade the number of obits in my file grew, then slowly I started to pull away. During that time, my grief for Alessandra shifted, somehow lessening my pull to record and connect with the recently deceased.

Chapter 2

Their Own Life and Death

My neighbourhood grocery store, having changed little over many years, appears outdated, verging toward dilapidation. Yet it's comfortable and an easy and known place to move around. When I arrived there on a recent morning, the entrance flowed more spaciously than it had the previous week when I shopped there last. Except for one check-out counter, the others had been dismantled, flipped into self-serve spaces. Shoppers were now expected to check themselves out while wondering whatever happened to their favourite cashier with whom over the years the habit of an effortless chat, the same smile, and "the sun's shining today, see you next week" comforted.

I should be used to it. My pharmacy manager wishes I would ignore the two remaining cashiers. My favourite bank teller stares at the bank's entrance as people visit the cash machine, no need to greet, no more hellos, no "nice day, although it might rain."

So much we do on our own. Some people draft their own obituary in anticipation of its appearance in one, or if they're lucky, two newspapers.

Two of my friends wrote their own. The first to die drafted a beautiful long essay about her loves, her dogs, her interests and her activism through the five decades she lived. It took up much space in two newspapers for three days and made for delightful reading. She confidently laid out who she believed she was, what she thought the world meant, and what she thought she meant to the world.

My second friend began her obituary seven years before she died. Periodically she made revisions to it and shared with me her additions and changes. After she died, none of us were able to find her obituary. Left with the uncertainty of whether she had at some point deleted it, the drafting task was finally turned over to a friend.

I haven't written mine, although leaving a family member or friend with this burden verges towards cruel. Laziness or the possibility that readers may complain that my obit appears self-serving, or boastful, or wearyingly self-effacing holds me back.

Regret Free

Those who have written their own obituary provide us with notes on living and dying free from regrets.

If I had known how long I'd live, I would have taken better care of myself.

At my age, I no longer buy green bananas!

I was a devoted daughter, sister, wife, colleague, engaged citizen, and loyal friend. I loved with my whole heart, sometimes winning and sometimes losing, but I don't regret trying. I had the luxury of being raised in a family where gender was not a limitation.

Well, after fighting three cancers, I fought as hard as I could, but I lost the battle. I'd rather be going to Aruba with my wife.

I've had a truly wonderful life with few regrets. What could be better than that?

It was a fun life so thanks for the times we had together! To those I did not get a chance to say goodbye to, my wish was to minimize the pain, especially for my family and so I wish for everyone to remember the good times we had together, maybe raise a glass of wine or beer, a cup of coffee, or tea for me.

Please find joy in the everyday, laugh often, be kind and take care of one another. Live each day as if it were your last. Find a way to do what makes you happy and surround yourself with those who lift you up.

Never forget this is your one precious life. There is nothing I love more than beautiful flowers, especially stargazer lilies. Floral donations are happily accepted. They will be donated to charity after my ceremony. Please plant a tree in my honour. Yellow birch is a favourite. Any tree would be simply amazing. I thank you for this.

I died at ninety-three, quite surprised to have made it to such an age. I look back and am thankful for a wonderful full life. Family and friends have been supportive through the ups and downs and music has been a constant in my life since I was twelve and joined a choir. It has been a joy and a comfort when times were tough. A celebration of my life (party!) will be held.

I, Christine, have written this about my life. The greatest moments of it all have been as a mother to my two wonderful daughters. I was extremely proud to earn my commission in the Canadian Women's Army Corps and to have served in the militia with the Royal Rifles of Canada. I have happy memories of being a girl guide leader. I've had a blessed life.

I finally joined Dana today, after gently slipping away peacefully in my sleep. I was ready—it was time to join him and all my dear friends. My nurses and doctors cared for me with gentle diligence and I am grateful to them. I leave with gratitude for a long life lived—so much dancing.

I had a passion for synchronized swimming and hockey.

b.1941. Well, I am leaving this world for a new adventure. I leave my partner who has lighted my life for my best thirty-seven years, my rock, my friend, my love. It was a great run, but I had to go. Thanks to all my friends and family who supported me through this wild period. A celebration of life will be held in the spring. Please remember to wear your bling. I love animals and children, and spent my last days at Hospice.

b.1951. Born at Banting Memorial Hospital, old site of Gander International airport. For those who loved, respected, believed in me, never let go of me, you were the reason for my forever smile and happiness. I will be that twinkling star far up in the sky, that tap on your shoulder, your Christmas angel. Please don't grieve for me. Just know I want nothing but happiness and good faith to follow you all, forever.

It is with great serenity that I inform you of my passing. I've had a truly wonderful life with few regrets. What could be better than that?

I thought I'd be around a lot longer.

Knitting with Mom, Doting on Dogs

1 deeply loved my parents; they were good people who were always there for me. Some of my best memories are of knitting with my mom. Like her, I loved to cook and bake. I loved cake with the perfect cup of tea. Have a sweet slice for me, now and again. Last but not least, I loved animals, especially dogs. I doted on those glorious creatures that gave me their unconditional love. King, Billy, Bailey, Ozzy, Jimmy, you taught me so much and made me happy. I was blessed to live a happy but simple life. I believed there is depth in the everyday, greatness in the simple and grace in the quiet.

b.1966. I leave this world too soon, but at peace. I leave behind my best friend and greatly loved big sister and my beloved wonder dog.

Remember My Fondness for Turtles and Smile—And Not Just Once

Writing their own last words, these autobiographers speak to us of who they were in the world, what held value for them, the meaning of their lives.

b.1952. Today I decided to seek for myself proof that Einstein had indeed nailed it with his theory of general relativity. Vivaldi's the Four Seasons provided music for the trip. Friends and family were by my side, as were memories of camping and canoe trips, diving from the dock, and fishing for salmon on the Miramichi. I'd like people to remember me for my diehard liberal political views, my fondness for turtles and frogs, my red leather jacket, and penchant for French manicures.

b.1942. If you are reading this then I have successfully transitioned to the next port of my journey. I have led a fulfilling life and am grateful for many accomplishments. My greatest goal was to ensure that my daughters become strong independent women. They have done that in spades. Keep an eye out for cardinals; yup, they will remind you of me. I enjoyed many things in my life. I gave it my best shot, but it was not to be.

b.1956. In my absence you are each tasked with helping other people smile. And I mean every day, not just once to placate the dead guy. Live your dream.

Please don't mourn me. I much prefer that you celebrate my life and the great times I enjoyed. Fortune smiled on me in my professional life in the RCAF. I have explored parts of six continents, missed Antarctica.

Oh, what a wonderful life I had! I got my social and playful nature from my crazy dad from Heart's Content, Newfoundland. I lost mum early. I loved horses, all animals really, and treasured many pets in my life. Met my first husband, a dashing pilot, and I loved to party and dance. Have to say I could light up a room! Do I have any advice for you based on how I lived my life? Be compassionate to people and animals, never miss a good party with friends, always stand by your kids and make them your priority, work hard when you have to, be proud of who you are and don't let people walk over you, let a smile light up your face as mine always did, and move on when it is time to do so, as I did on July 6.

Chapter 3

Talking to the Dead

Put some life into the obits!
—Arthur Hueston, publisher, *Aylmer Express*

This book celebrates obituaries—it celebrates those who dared defy conventions, who lived during ways of life now disappeared, whose lives counted on their terms, who experienced extreme situations, and those whose contexts were most fortunate. And it celebrates obituarists, perhaps untrained and first time as obituarist, unwillingly taking on the task. In the tailspin of their grief, obituarists often dive in deep to draft within a short span of time the core of a life.

Writing an obit can be a confidence-breaking experience, writing the essence of the life of a person close to you, with whom three days ago you might have shared a meal or a joke or a game of pool. Perhaps the obit writer drafts amidst a sense of undone-ness submerged within an unlifting fog. Concentration challenges and the sudden newness of this world minus the person who has just died, can falter assuredness.

Obituarists write a life in the past tense—and the counting of years and the counting of obituary words, each one a cost. The telling, what goes in, what stays out, where certain hints lay.

The arc, the awkwardness of the beginning, who justifies their name included. The terrible decisions of the middle: who was she really? The reveal or not, perhaps the safety of facts, feeling removed. Then the thanking: a caregiver, a nurse, a doctor in her life for only two months, yet noted. And the final: please donate to what cause, what organization, and the where, when of getting together to what? Celebrate? Mourn? Remember? All new. The loss, the partially told life, slanted.

Eupeptic Send-Offs, Lighthearted Goodbyes

Henry, you now can put the newspaper away. Your name is in the obits today.

Mom, this is a hard day for us as we have to say goodbye to you. We're going to miss your look when we broke your etiquette rules and heard you say "I didn't raise you girls that way!" However, we won't miss the numerous calls about a missing cell phone and a TV remote that refused to work. We want to thank you for leaving us an endless supply of knick-knacks that we will fight over to see who ends up with the most, game on.

Dear GG, thank you for the chocolate chip cookies and for scrabble at sunrise. Thank you for reminding us to turn off the lights and for your mutual fund advice. Goodnight GG. Sleep well.

Food fights and pies in the face won't be as much fun without you, but the tradition will continue!

Off you go to the back forty now. Don't forget your packed lunch.

So when the sun paints the sky in the west at the end of the day, we will stand on the shore of the lake and remember you. See you later Dad.

I hope you are walking along a beach at sunset, feeling the sand between your toes.

Born in Newfoundland, he was the loudest human being ever. He was not a patient man. His wife was a bloody saint. He called me incessantly, dropped by unexpectedly far too frequently. You either loved him or not so much, and he was fine with that. His last day was like any day before. Wake up, create noise, make many, many phone calls, create more noise, have dinner. The end came quick, just as he always hoped for. If we could be as lucky to have the exact last day to do exactly as we wanted. My phone isn't blowing up anymore because you're calling, and I never thought I would miss that so much.

He would be the first to raise a gin and tonic to his extraordinary life.

Here's to her, who always flipped straight to the obituaries and is finally here herself. Her delight for life took her many places. She was an enigma. She died of lung cancer. She wants you to know she finally quit smoking.

b.1951. I'm ignoring my dear sister's request. She departed on her own terms, as usual. Good-bye, rest well, you've earned it.

He took his last drive down the country road and past the old homestead to his final resting place in the cemetery.

He was world-renowned for his lack of patience with stupid people. We had to refuse his request to have him standing in a corner of the room holding a Coors light. But next time you're at your local watering hole, OVER TIP and raise a glass in honour of him.

He requested to be sent off in the Irish way, with drinks, family, and friends.

He fixed his last car and hung up his wrench.

She'll be remembered for her blunt honesty and her fighting spirit.

To honour him, put on an old plaid shirt, grab a beer, and let the sounds of a Rolling Stones song take you away.

He was always the last person to leave the party.

May she be at peace with her father and her beloved dog, Ginger. We will toast our memories of her with a Heineken.

Died at home. It was the first and last time she didn't have an opinion on a matter.

May we all know the strength he demonstrated in the face of cruel adversity that robbed him of his legs but never his spirit. Each day we, his friends, grieve our loss and cheer our good fortune for having known him. We'll see you on the other side.

Exchanged the mortal realm for the invisible realms. Remaining on the earth plane in varying stages of health, confusion, and grief are his wife, sister, son, and daughter. A cremation is pending. A celebration will be held with him as the guest of honour. In the interim, please commit many random acts of kindness to the unsuspecting in memory of him.

He had numerous close calls, including near drownings, axe throwing accidents and chopping down trees with his brother at the top of the tree.

She read obits. In fact, she would have read this one.

His favorite pastime was slamming drawers while quietly swearing under his breath. A Canadiens fan, he shouted at the television on Saturday nights.

The Deceased's Wishes

In his organizational binder, Paul wanted his obit to say he died from eating too many cookies washed down with rye at the age of one hundred. But at eighty-eight it was from complications following a couple of falls. He wrote he'd be deeply missed and lovingly remembered by his children. He did not want money spent on a rehash of his long life, so instead join us at a visitation.

A rebel in his own way, he joined the navy at seventeen, which was itself an act of rebellion as far as his parents were concerned. He loved muscle cars and motorcycles. He was a practical and pragmatic man. He would have believed that his obituary had already gone on far too long. Get on with it he would say.

He made a specific request that we donate to a homeless shelter as he believed everyone deserves a good meal and a safe refuge. Predeceased by his parents and his loyal canine companion.

b.1943. My beautiful, vivacious wife of fifty-three years has died, a casualty of lung cancer for which a lifelong smoking habit was probably a contributing factor. The last week was very difficult for her but perhaps a blessing that it was relatively short under the circumstances.

She was the love child of two members of the armed services. Not long after her birth, she was adopted and renamed. She was passionate about everything in which she was involved, family, friends, horses, dogs, and herself. She asked that I say goodbye for her to her friends, her supportive AA buddies, her extended family, including her children. A celebration of life will be held in the not-too-distant future when the weather is more suitable to her taste and enjoyment.

If family and friends wish to remember him, he would like you to go and play a game of golf.

The Anti-Obit

Always a touch backlogged with his projects, he postponed publication of his obituary as long as he could before the accumulation of aging's downsides finally overwhelmed his constitution.

Years ago, he wrote "no death notice." This is a life notice.

Let's skip the obituary. He wants you to wear bright and cheery clothes to his remembrance service.

He requested no service in his memory. His ashes will be spread as per his last wishes. A private man who lived a quiet life. He lived and died on his own terms.

The Recognition, the Commemoration

Recognition—a scholarship in the name of the deceased, a ghost bike tied to a fence, teddy bears, toys and flowers on a sidewalk, an annual fundraiser for a cause, a newly planted tree, perhaps a hardy highbush cranberry shrub, or a plaque affixed to a bench in a park by a river.

Commemoration—a funeral with incense, a sermon, hymns; a memorial full of stories, remembering. The deceased may attend, body in casket or ashes in urn, or not attend at all. Perhaps a quickly crafted ceremony, a celebration of a life, a wake, a religious service or not, a party, perhaps festivities at the local community centre, a gathering at a pub for a pint or two, or a private, intimate occasion, perhaps a dinner. Any of these may include photos, videos, memorabilia, songs that resonate, all tidbits of a life.

Not everyone is noticed officially after death and not everyone's death is marked by a memorializing event. Some have it said in their obits that they don't want a special event: *Nothing, thank you.*

Dressing for the Event and What to Expect

Those attending the service are encouraged to wear their running shoes in memory of his love of running, the times when he felt most at peace and to wear blue—not black.

Dress code casual at her request.

A celebration of his life in true hunter style. If you have camo attire, wear it... and send flowers! He loved them, lots of them!

No formal funeral wear please. His preference was to have a party—preferably with him present, but alternatively, raise a glass on his behalf.

Join the family and enjoy a good chuckle while remembering him. What a character he was!

Please greet the family at the reception after the service.

In keeping with her character, there will be no memorial service: she encouraged us to remember her with no fuss.

There will be no speeches at her service.

He will rest at the funeral home. A celebration of his life at the curling club. A ceremony will take place in the spring, the time of renewal and lilacs.

And some families advise that they will commemorate privately, in their own way.

Done Lists and To-Do Lists

Each of my days carries its own to-do list, completed items periodically checked off. And each day I have items that roll over to the next, although some items stay on the list until rendered outdated, transforming as they disappear into a likely-never-will-get-to-them category.

And my list of some-day goals each juggle with my vision of my future self. All look forward.

But obituaries faithfully look backwards. Rarely is a project mentioned that a deceased person never realized or regretted never undertaking. The retrospective features: the to-do list simply deleted. The unresolved, untouched, or not yet completed goals and hopes omitted from the obituary. Unaccomplished projects, the question of what a person did not yet achieve or take part in now of small concern—except for the obits of young people, whose obits mention potential, a struck potential. These youth on the edge of blossoming, about to touch success, beckon us to envision their imagined future.

Some obits, though, do point to a to-do list for families and friends.

She passed away on her own terms and with her brilliant sense of timing. As a result of World War Two, she developed wanderlust and a willingness to take risks. She loved live theatre. Take someone to a show or bring them flowers. She would like that. Enjoy the sunrise.

b.1970. She met her death with equanimity. As a teenager, she spent one formative year as a member of the L'Arche community. Please hug someone you love.

Her father was a farm worker in Scotland. Her ashes will be returned to Scotland to join her mother in Ayrshire. You can celebrate her life with a wee dram of single malt scotch, or if you'd rather, some Croft's sherry, and tell a story about her.

We will raise a glass of Keith's in his honour.

Verbs for Death, Adjectives for Loss

They've passed, passed on, passed away, died, gone from us, gone to join their mother, father, sister, infant son. Reunited with their partners, flown to Heaven.

They've rendered us shocked and stunned. They've left us with gratitude or with resentment, left us to mourn, left us bereft.

Their Terms

As she waved her last cheery goodbye, she did so knowing she would be missed. She died on her own resolute terms.

A believer that all good things must come to an end, he passed away as he wished.

When told that his request to die under the MAID (medical assistance in dying) program would be granted, he replied with his favourite refrain, Hallelujah. An artist, a soldier, philosopher, an author, scavenger, sculptor, a husband, father and grandfather.

Facing the final curtain, he chose to leave us on his own terms. Still doing back flips off the diving board into his eighties. His jokes are not to be forgotten. We hope you will toast him with a martini or scotch and maybe a good cigar.

Fifty-seven years. Departed on the day of his choosing, ending a life-altering dance with ALS. An inveterate salesman with a love of telling stories, repeated endlessly, his brown eyes laughing. He asserted that he had lived the life he wanted—a bodybuilder with unfailing optimism.

b.1932. She died with the same sense of adventure and determination by which she lived her life. She ended her fight with cerebellar ataxia with the help of medical assistance in dying. In the Yukon, she became an early proponent and lifelong lover of the Yukon Quest dog sled race.

b.1938. She left us as she lived life: in full control having chosen an assisted death after raging against cancer for too long. Relieved that the law allowed her this choice, but angry that she was forced to leave while she had cognition. She loved nature, the moon, animals, power tools, and a select group of humans.

Stricken with the same serious illness his mother had suffered from, he left the hospital and ceased treatment. Since he had always lived life his way, to no one's surprise he chose to end it on his own terms. Happy to be home, he spent some time watching a hockey game, then went to bed and simply stopped breathing. Given up for adoption and adopted at three, he always wanted to do things his way.

Died at the time of his choosing in the company of loved ones. His struggle with ALS was marked by dignity, clear-eyed courage, and courtesy, with his subversive wit always at the ready.

She accepted life and the afterlife equally as part of the same cosmic plan. Passed away on her own terms.

It's not MAID's fault that he was early for every appointment and so died just hours before the doctor arrived.

b.1954. On his terms, exercising his right to die with dignity.

Departure

Obits describe death as a gateway, a flight, a boat voyage, a departure to somewhere, a journey to the next and usually final place.

b.1958. She had been fighting an uninvited virus that climbed aboard during one of her jaunts on Royal Caribbean. Having time to contemplate her compromised condition, I believe that she was ready to resign her role in "The Great Adventure." She was confident in Christ's promised relocation offer and has accepted his new assignment with great joy. She now runs the Angels R Us Travel kiosk in Heaven.

He slipped away from port on his final voyage in these waters.

She is continuing her journey from this realm to the next.

He will probably eat a Big Mac on his way to Heaven.

He boarded his final flight at the age of eighty-two. He lived his passion for flying and exploring the world. A pilot with RCAF, he enjoyed jigsaw puzzles, all things German, sweets, especially bridge mixtures. His final voyage takes him to a comfy La-Z-Boy recliner.

He sailed into the sunset for the last time leaving his crew on the jetty.

He is out of the office, boarded the boat, and gone fishing.

He worked on the Canadarm with the NRC Aerospace Centre and now he has reached his highest place possible.

She left this earth.

He departed on his last flight to his final destination.

He is sailing now on fair seas, the wind at his back, and a smile on his face.

An opera singer and world traveller, she took her final voyage into the arms of her beloved Saviour.

He crossed his final finish line with a time of eighty-seven years, 264 days. He trained as a physiotherapist, although his real passion was football (soccer on this side of the ocean). He discovered running in the mid 1970s and marathons became his passion. He ran 45 of them before hanging up his shoes.

Our father would like to announce his departure on a very special trip. We wish him safe and happy travels.

He loved planes and has flown off to join his daughter.

We wish her a joyful journey.

You are now free to fly.

Maybe now he will get that hole in one.

An avid traveller, he left for his last voyage at seventy-one years of age.

The sun broke through the clouds, and he was liberated to the skies.

> There are more things in heaven and earth than
> have ever been dreamt of.
> —Hamlet

Arrival to Where They Are, What They're Doing

In another dimension now, enjoying his father and grandfather.

His spirit is probably travelling beyond time and space.

To us, her children, she is now our sun, our moon, and our stars.

As the scientist in Dad pointed out, our composition only changes at death and our energy remains indestructible forever.

Dad lives eternally both in our hearts and in the universe. No rocket ship required, Dad.

After a long battle with life and pain, she finished her battles and changed dimensions.

He passed into spirit.

He loved to read fantasy and heroic quests exploring the universe. We envision him as having arrived at "the shores of the outer sea" (Lord of the Rings).

She has gone to a better place to meet our daughter and many four-legged friends.

Surrounded by family who helped him find his way to the Big Sea.

She was her husband's touchstone without whom his life would have been incomplete. Her ashes will be in the wind with her husband's after his death.

He has returned home.

He crossed over to the next stage of our human experience.

Our dad was a man of annoying consistency. He's gone to share a cherry pie with mum. Our parents used to say the key to longevity was their desire to outlive each other and inherit everything.

Dressed in his favourite plaid shirt, a book under his arm and a picture of his daughter, he said his last good byes. By now he is sitting at the end of a dock with the love of his life, him with his beer, her with her red wine, smiling down on all the people they love.

She is thankfully reunited with her sister.

She is with our dad, having a martini and a game of bridge with her lifelong friends.

He joined his wife for their first of many dinner parties in the sky.

At the age of one hundred, our mom joined those gone before and is no doubt tripping the light fantastic with the man of her dreams. Born in County Cork, gone to join the party and sing and dance her heart away.

She will oversee her grandchildren's milestones from afar.

He lost the love of his life too early. And he waited and waited for her to come to him. With the spring, he hoped she would appear. And she did. They are together now.

She has gone to find her mother and her father on the other side of the moon.

He is reunited with his beloved first wife. Predeceased by his second wife.

She is now busy getting things organized.

She is safe in Richard's loving arms.

He is free of the pain of cluster headaches he endured for twenty years and is breathing effortlessly. His best pal, his dog, is curled up at his feet as he chats with those who have gone before him.

Passed away peacefully to join her beloved for their wedding anniversary.

He will undoubtedly be welcomed on the other side with love and a party.

He was born at sunrise, forty years ago, and died at sunset. His pal, Penny, is waiting to welcome him to Heaven.

b.1947. An exceptional man has journeyed forth, surrounded by his loved ones as he peacefully transitioned into the heavens.

He will join his two sons.

The Great Slopes of Heaven

The thought of Dad welcoming her to Heaven with rousing polka music on the accordion.

Her transition to Heaven was made easier knowing that she will be reunited with her son and grandson.

b.1950. He left this world after a tough illness to ski the great slopes of Heaven.

He touched the face of God at the age of seventeen.

She slipped into the hands of God.

They are now together holding hands and dancing in Heaven.

He was welcomed into the arms of our Lord at sunrise.

He looked at life as a race well run and at death as simply the highly anticipated reunion with the saviour of his soul.

We rejoice that he is now and forever in the arms of the angels.

Her canoe slipped peacefully into the heavenly waters accompanied by her Jesus, the holy spirit, and surrounded by her family, friends, and love.

She sends heavenly hugs to her friends.

God has released her spirit.

Called home to Heaven in his eighty-first year. We miss him already.

Chapter 4

Who They Are

I talk with Maureen, my friend and fellow obituary reader, about obits: trends that week or a surprising, odd, or fascinating obit. But they aren't always like that. When I said to her "The obits have been dull recently. I wish they'd perk up," we paused, holding that remark in the air.

The Adventurers among Us

b.1927. She loved to play cards, especially bridge. She was an awful cook and her family were the guinea pigs for her experiments. Her children all acquired an appreciation for steak, fish, and vegetables after leaving home. She snorkelled in her seventies even though she couldn't swim and was terrified of water. At seventy-seven, she ran her first five-kilometre race in forty-four minutes.

What a life! Sky diving at ninety, skiing at ninety-five. His many talents included wind surfing, unicycling, juggling, poker, gymnastics, and ear wiggling. He had been in a submarine, had climbed to base camp of Mount Everest, and was shipwrecked in Antarctica.

A proud Bear Clan member of the Oneida Nation. He was never lost, always found a different direction to his destination, even if it meant turning around.

b.1930. He was a diver and swimmer and known for diving off the bridges around the city—and he shouldn't have done that. He loved driving a Zamboni.

Scuba diving at the Great Barrier Reef and enjoying disc jockeying, he'll be forever admired for the courage he demonstrated in light of the special challenges throughout his life.

b.1945. The list of adventures he pursued in his life—hiking at Lake O'Hara, paddling the Nahanni River, ski touring and sea kayaking in Greenland, and hiking around Mont Blanc. An interest in photography blossomed into a full-blown obsession, leading to early morning escapades chasing snowy owls or late-night attempts to capture the Milky Way. He spent good times hiking through his partner's native country and he succeeded in learning the language of that country.

She enjoyed encountering animals in the wild, kayaking with whales on both coasts, meeting bears and elk on hikes through the Rockies, mingling with the massive migrating herds and their predators on the Serengeti. She was a bit of a daredevil and was usually the first in her family to undertake risky activities, whether trying out exotic culinary dishes or off-trail adventures or hanging off the CN Tower.

Travellers

Ninety-four years. Lifelong horse racing fan, he rarely missed attending the Kentucky Derby and the Queen's Plate.

One hundred years. She drove her car from Florida at ninety-four. At ninety-nine, she flew back from Florida on her own.

He had a passion for thoroughbred horses and when travelling always made sure there was a racetrack nearby.

She made many birding trips to various parts of the world and was excited to share her experiences with others.

She loved ice cream, dogs, babies, and travel anywhere, particularly in winter.

Eighty-two years. For his eightieth birthday we walked the Camino de Santiago together.

A passion for cycling, he cycled to Florida.

A satellite communications engineer. At fifty-two, he followed his dream of completing a university degree in music. He cycled across the Andes from Argentina to Chile and hiked the Akshayuk Pass in Baffin Island.

He played Pokémon at ten and so fell in love with Japan, where he moved to as an adult.

b.1926. She spent two years sailing throughout the Caribbean on the trip of a lifetime.

A singular man, everything he did, he approached as an explorer, a sleuth, a student. His curiosity just had no off switch. For the past twenty-five years he had been taking friends and family on incredible wilderness adventures on Canada's northern rivers. He did academic studies on Chinese foot binding, medicine related to the American Civil War, and Hong Kong Canadian prisoners of war. Born in Winnipeg, his childhood was a typical depression-era upbringing.

His passion for sailing culminated with a transatlantic crossing with his two sons.

In retirement, he cycled across Australia and New Zealand. In his nineties, he wrote three books.

Games and Sports

She became an avid golfer although wisely never kept score.

Interested in cryptic crosswords and current events, she was known to put the world on hold every year during Wimbledon. The epitome of style and grace.

She was a pitcher, a lifeguard, and competed in doubles canoeing.

Growing up in India, he enjoyed big game hunting.

As a teen, he was a pitcher for a softball team.

Forty-nine years. He was a devoted gym rat. He loved rollerblading and nightlife with friends.

He completed ten marathons and rode his bike thirty-five kilometers each day to and from work.

b.1923. She promoted Junior Girls Golf.

His mind was made to be an excellent bridge player.

b.1933. He was proud of the four holes in one he made during his golfing days.

b.1961. She spent many years playing in a fast pitch league.

b.1954. A passion for motor racing. He loved to talk about his own racing days, when as a young man he raced a Honda civic in a dedicated Honda series. He loved dinner on the deck with good wine and lots of dogs, followed by an evening cruise on his pontoon.

She participated in the Special Olympics.

She carried throughout her life a deep fondness for water, swimming, ice skating, and family.

Ninety-five years. She was regularly seen in the neighbourhood on her daily six kilometre walk along the river.

She went up in a hot air balloon in her eighties because—why not?

He was a fast walker and a snooker player.

Gliding was a big part of her life and she flew open cockpit gliders in competitions.

He spent many years drag car racing, stock car racing, and go-cart racing. Loved darts and poker.

An unbeatable chess player.

A fierce scrabble player, an attentive aunt, and a loving lifelong companion to her sister.

A competitive game-player, she spent countless hours with friends and family challenging rules and winning.

A tough competitor at cards. A wannabe great curler.

An undisputed trivia king.

b.1935. A competitive yacht racer, he enjoyed the win and was always one to run a tight ship and a clean deck.

b.1925. Her strong character, forged in Saskatchewan during the Depression, impelled her to persist through both the good and the bad times. She used her quick wit to her advantage. One of her favorite pastimes was euchre, a game at which she was very competitive.

Our memory is a more perfect world than the universe:
it gives back life to those who no longer exist.
—Guy de Maupassant

Word Lovers

She was a stickler for grammar and loved cryptic crosswords. She read the newspaper with a red pen. Her memory for detail was remarkable.

A passion for reading, especially books on war history, espionage, or anything he could put his hands on.

He always addressed people by their names, which he was careful to remember. A prolific maker of lists, lover of words, word play, opera, songs, and singers.

b.1929. A gift for reciting poetry. With his steamboat, he participated in an annual steamboat flotilla.

Her love of numbers and beautiful penmanship was an asset for her job as an accounts payable clerk.

Ninety-two years. She was a devotee of the written word, the CBC and the New York Times crosswords in pen! Immaculate handwritten notes.

Sixty-five years. A stalwart defender of the Oxford comma and a fanatical devotee of Monty Python. He could recite the major Monty Python skits from memory to the delight or chagrin of friends and family.

Wife of a farmer, cattle buyer, and auctioneer. She loved exchanging letters and at a young age won a penmanship award.

A member of the Bliss Carman Society.

A lover of books and a properly made cup of tea. She retired from a department store.

Born with a pencil in her hand, she was an artist, writer, and poet.

Ninety-six years. A trivia buff, a lover of birds and flowers and known especially for her roast beef dinners. Proper grammar was a necessity. Died after a life filled with love.

b.1931. She was a prolific reader of Nurse Betty books and an okay cook, as her understanding of recipe ingredients was creative.

A self-styled storyteller and poet, he mc'd family weddings and office parties. Played Santa Claus and Bozo the clown at functions.

He would only tackle the most difficult crosswords.

She loved ballet, genealogy, and had an addiction to murder mysteries.

She could shred crossword puzzles, devour books, and breeze through a game of Trivial Pursuit while doing a Rubik's Cube puzzle.

b.1988. She was a natural writer who gleefully put in the requisite ten thousand hours to develop her voice. Incapable of passing a homeless person without sharing whatever she had.

Her elevated curiosity combined with a passion for reading resulted in wide ranging discussions including etymological origins and world religions.

Funny People

We had a lifetime worth of his corny jokes.

Eighty-four years. He spent his spare time as a slightly dyslexic lawn care failure, wooden boat builder, latterly a radio-controlled model boat sailor, gadget fan, Economist reader, worrier, and a general distraction to those close to him.

His pranks and ability to fix or build nearly anything.

b.1975. A joke teller and book devourer, he kept us laughing until the end, somehow ensuring our comfort as well. He always wanted to take the longest and most scenic route. He loved to linger and cook and gather people at his table. A person of full presence, he paid close attention.

He always had a way to fix any problem even if it was downright dangerous to his health.

Her years were filled with lots of activities—sewing, knitting, cheating at board games.

Known for his sense of humour but not his dancing, he always wished he had done comedy at an open mic night.

Her sense of humour kept everyone from taking themselves too seriously.

He shared his love of nature and the outdoors with our children, teaching them to canoe, kayak, and fish. He loved puns and had a squinty-eyed laugh that was loudest at his own groaner jokes.

A popular hairstylist until health issues ended her career. Although she took the loss of her parents very hard, she never lost her wicked sense of humor.

Eighty-two years. He was happiest golfing and playing darts. His passions included communicating with his CB radio buddies, woodworking, painting virtually everything in sight, and he will be remembered for holding court as a master story teller whose embellishments were legend.

Hunt Camps and Kayaks

She had more than a four-decade association with a hunt club.

She taught her grandchildren about the wonders of a turtle returning year after year to lay her eggs. In spring, she pointed out the many varieties of wildflowers. She loved the seasons of the year, fed chipmunks and hummingbirds, attracted butterflies and moths to her garden with special plantings. Fed chickadees and dog sledded in her eighties.

In Switzerland, he fell in love with mountains. He was never happier than when off somewhere in the Rockies with a high fly rod and a pair of hip waders. In retirement, he and his wife restored a historic property in the town of Bonavista and spent evenings watching icebergs in the bay.

A beekeeper, he passed away while tending to his many hives.

His most cherished memories were gained far from human settlement, often in a dog sled or a canoe.

She was an amateur geologist, ornithologist, naturalist, and archeologist. Friend of all chipmunks and wildlife.

He said his best education came from our natural world.

She was an artist and a birder.

Although allergic to bees, he kept hives in various locations.

He loved the spectacular view of the harbour from his condo and spent many happy hours gazing out the window watching the ferries, boats, and floatplanes come and go. He never lost his sense of wonder in these everyday occurrences or in the huge advancements that he witnessed over the course of his lifetime.

In his younger days, he spent weeks camping and eating out at many different establishments.

b.1962. She lived for her flute, her singing, her stained glass, her kayak and cottage and enjoyed all the world had to offer.

Accomplished mix of McGyver, Red Green, and Grizzly Adams, he preferred coexisting with nature over dominating it. An inventive tinkerer, a master woodsman. Annual solo wilderness forays, adored provider of peanuts and tamer of blue jays and chipmunks, crafty schemer, and perpetrator of practical jokes.

She made a good choice in the person she married. She loved nature and went on camping trips with her father, with whom she shared a special bond.

He never missed an opportunity to go to the hunt camp even though he never fished or hunted.

Loving Food: Chefs, Bakers, and Foodies

Because of him, his family enjoyed three vegetables at every meal.

She spoiled her family with perogies and cabbage rolls.

A man who loved to make people laugh, eat great food, and drink even greater wine.

Unfailing provider of fresh baked goods and tea.

Loved cooking, reading, playing cards, travelling, art, puzzles, and always being right!

She was a perfectionist and a superb home cook. She learned Lebanese cooking from her mother-in-law and her signature dishes were without equal.

She was an exuberant lady who loved her aquafit friends. We will miss your baking, knitting, and your unique way of expressing yourself.

He loved his before-dinner drink.

Supplied tomatoes to friends and neighbours from his fifty tomato plants.

b.1950. He enjoyed good food and wine and speaking French, his mother tongue. A lifelong passion for military history.

She became a vegan at a time when that was considered odd.

A dedicated hobbyist, he never did anything by half measure. In his nineties, he demonstrated a flair for cooking.

Pancake maker extraordinaire.

The universe will always be much richer than our ability to understand it.
—Carl Sagan

Intellectuals and Their Interests

b.1946. A coffeeshop intellectual, he created a tight-knit community of debaters, jokers, and troublemakers at his local coffeeshop.

The entire cosmos fascinated him. He loved learning and laughing.

Ninety-three years. She left the farm in Manitoba and graduated with an MA in math at a time when women in universities were much less common.

Years of vigorous debating. Hobby farming.

An interest in astronomy and theology.

She proudly graduated from university with her BA after twenty years of night classes, all the while running a household and raising three children. As a teenager, she and two girlfriends drove across the country.

She was intellectually ahead of her time and a forward thinker.

A proud university graduate at the age of eighty.

A recent convert to Qi Gong, an enthusiastic learner of Spanish.

She pursued a study of Buddhism.

b.1951. A passionate military historian, his tireless research breathed new life into the artifacts he collected. His second love was the revered hunt camp where he would share a few pints and stories with pals, faithfully, every year.

His unique "out of the box" thinking.

Classic Rock, Bach, and Bagpipes

b.1948. She was a violinist, a tap dancer, a steeple chase runner, a model, a linguist.

b.1993. She had a particular fondness for classic rock. She could be found at every vinyl record show across the city, haggling with dealers for the best possible deal on a Pink Floyd or a Led Zeppelin record. Her life philosophy can be summed up as "I travel the world to pet all the cats."

Her love of old-time fiddling was a highlight in her life.

He played weird instruments in various bands. His loves included Elvis Presley and WW2 books.

He rarely missed a day playing the piano for his own amusement.

b.1933. A bagpiper, he played and toured with the RAF Pipe Band. He taught the pipes for years.

At thirteen, she started playing the organ at church.

She brightened the lives of thousands with countless accordion concerts. She could play anything and she loved whimsical art.

Played trombone in the school band.

A proud Maritimer. Missed by former daughter-in-law and former son-in-law, she could not be beat at Scrabble despite many valiant attempts by her children. Always singing or humming a tune, her favourites, It's a Long Way to Tipperary and My Bonnie Lies Over the Ocean.

He will be remembered for his devotion to the music of Bach. Well cultured and regarded as a scholarly gentleman, he enjoyed musical concerts.

His passion for country music will live forever in his heart.

After a well celebrated life, the crane has landed. The music stopped. He had a love for country music and met most of the best—Johnny Cash, Waylon Jennings, Rosanne Cash, and Willie Nelson.

He laughed loudly and loved to sing, although without any sense of pitch.

101 years. In her old age, she remembered songs from the twenties, thirties, and forties. Now she will be reunited with the long-departed childhood friend who she grew up with in that era.

b.1934. Fond of operatic music and works from the Baroque period. He played the recorder in an amateur music group.

Ninety-two years. She enjoyed attending Shriners events. Loved opera, bus tours to New York's Metropolitan Opera, and music appreciation classes.

He loved all types of music, the Beatles being his favourite.

Dedicated to music, played the violin, mandolin, and ukulele. He climbed the Pyrenees in France.

She had perfect pitch. Quite possibly Roger Federer's biggest fan.

b.1945. He went to Woodstock and attended plenty of concerts over the years. A trip down memory lane will be held at the tavern.

Sixty-three years. A synchronized swimmer, a swimming instructor, and lifeguard. She obtained grade ten in piano from the Royal Conservatory of Music. She was a free spirit and a voracious reader.

Cutting a Rug

And boy, could he dance. A talented ballroom dancer, he was also well bred.

Irish to the core, she could dance quite the jig.

Learned square dance calling at age thirteen and did it until a few months before his death.

b.1930. She was married for twenty-five years to a Scottish-born singer extraordinaire. Her feet loved to dance to the tunes of Elvis or tap to a down east fiddler.

Seventy-four years. Born in Yugoslavia, he participated in many international tours for his church choir and folk dancing.

We are a landscape of all we have seen.
—Isamu Noguchi, sculptor and architect

Sculptors, Carvers, Painters, Vintage Trucks, and Gramophones

She enjoyed painting with neighbours, as evidenced by the number of her oil paintings hanging throughout the house.

Because of an accident, he became quadriplegic. He lived independently and painted with his mouth.

He was an ace wood duck carver.

He fashioned sculptures with fossil stones.

He had a great passion for cars, and he must surely hold the world record for how many he owned during his lifetime.

A darts player and stamp collector.

A collector of antiques, gramophones being his specialty.

A devoted collector of unicorns.

A collector of vintage trucks.

He nurtured a love of stamp collecting.

A rock collector.

He was a collector of curling pins and other curling memorabilia from clubs right across Canada and the US.

Collector of pig paraphernalia, African violets, and all things purple.

Madly Off in All Directions

Had many hobbies including flying and crashing his radio-controlled airplanes.

Philatelist. Numismatist. Clock maker. Serial traveller. Intricate needlepoint artist. Serious recycler. Model train enthusiast. Wine maker.

Fun dad. Wise dad. Fair dad. Tough dad. He loved the law, history, golf, boats, autumn colours, spontaneous digressions down country roads, oysters, anything sweet, and single malt scotch.

She was an extreme frugality practitioner.

He enjoyed the finer things in life: auto repairs, coin collecting, stock trading, and science fiction movies.

A farm boy, a coach, a paddler, a poet, singer, a banjo player, teacher, a philosopher, a traveller, a storyteller.

b.1955. A race walker with a talent for entertaining. Whether playing music, imitating accents, doing impersonations, or skits, he was a one man show to the delight of everyone who knew him.

Logophile, bibliophile, audiophile, botanophile, anglophile, thalassaphile, ornithophile, ailurophile, and Christian. Retired textbook editor.

In summer he jet-skied, and in winter he skidooed, four-wheeled, and ice fished. An inventor, he built a 1931 Chevy, which garnered the adoration of anyone who laid eyes on it.

He loved jazz and hanging out with his friends at his local pub.

Failing eyesight sadly reduced his research capacity. His love of Persian carpets, on which he was considered a leading expert, never dimmed.

A member of a gliding club where he was a flight instructor.

Loved his wine and mushroom picking.

Sixty-one years. He fought cancer three times, determined to stay for his family, but couldn't.

Loved Led Zeppelin, Jimi Hendrix, Irish castles. His gym became his second home, he indulged in tattoos, he looked imposing but wasn't.

He personified the true hippie, keeping his long blond hair to the end, smoking his little pipe daily, and always spreading his words of peace and love. Loved pool and darts.

b.1933. Passionate about growing cacti, searching Tuscan hills for Etruscan art, watching foreign films, supporting human rights, combing the beach for shells, practising yoga, and voraciously reading.

A lifelong marijuana advocate, he would certainly have enjoyed the poetic symmetry in Canada's plan to legalize cannabis two days after what would have been his eighty-fourth birthday.

Loved the Young and the Restless, bath products, fine beer, strong coffee.

Years of scrabble games, movie nights, and rosé wine. A sophisticated and stunning woman, she turned heads and hearts wherever she went.

He was blessed with the ability to build or fix anything, hunt, fish, and bake.

He will be remembered for his love of a beach, a good newspaper, and a gin and tonic.

b.1928. Remembered by all her friends at the casino and the OLG slots.

Simple Pleasures and Giving Back

Four-year-old Renata, brightly new to Canada, stood near me by a grocery store's bins of nuts, seeds, and dried fruit. With a swoosh, an employee appeared telling her to move away. A week later, in the large foyer of a modern professional building, a security officer lurched towards her, "Get away, move."

At ten, twelve, fourteen, sixteen, and beyond, she was trailed in stores by security guards who did so without surreptitiousness. When with her, I watched each man, so close behind my daughter's neck, behind her every step, her every turn into a new aisle.

Older, while driving my car, police stopped her claiming a need to confirm identification, proof of ownership, assurance that she wasn't driving a stolen vehicle.

Her choice: she turned to adulthood kindly, no storm waiting to thunder.

The choices we make. How we live. How we give back.

For twenty years once a week, she was at the Salvation Army hostel at 7:00 a.m. serving breakfast.

A social guy, he volunteered in a therapeutic riding group and participated in several bowling leagues.

A strong-willed woman, she supported those with special needs through wheelchair tennis and guide dogs for the blind. A palpable sense of service, high standards. Dry sense of humour.

He invented gadgets no one will ever use.

Baptized in the Miramichi River, he enjoyed mum's one-of-a-kind, tasty molasses cookies, and fishing and snowshoeing.

He loved being Santa Claus, completing fourteen years at the mall.

She grew up on her granny's farm. Bagpipes were part of the musical entertainment and family gatherings. She and her two sisters enjoyed playing with their pet turtles and roller skating. Her weekly allowance was twenty-five cents and they bought dairy milk chocolate, tootsie rolls, jaw breakers, black balls, and juicy fruit gum. She took shortcuts to school over farmland belonging to a farmer rumoured to have a shotgun waiting for any kid who dared take this route. Mum wrapped pennies and nickels and dimes in tin foil and hid them in birthday cakes. She ate butterscotch lifesavers on the ferry to prevent seasickness.

He had a great interest in South America and an affection for Rio.

He often stopped for coffee at his favourite diner.

He had so many fond memories of family ties at the cottage, especially the mandatory daily bowl of porridge.

She loved shopping the day away.

His hobby was growing Christmas trees.

Proud of his 1957 Chevy.

An instructor to blind bowlers, she faced her last days with humour and dignity.

A volunteer with prisoner rehabilitation programs.

A quilter and rug hooker, she grew African violets to give to shut ins.

She volunteered at the neonatal intensive care unit and never hesitated to hold a stranger's baby at a restaurant so a mom could have her meal.

After her husband died, she rekindled a long-ago friendship with another man.

A volunteer guide at the Canadian War Museum.

She dedicated years to volunteering with several organizations.

One hundred years. She drove arthritic patients to clinics and ran the hospital flower shop.

He was a life-long canvasser for the Kidney Foundation.

A founding member of a shelter for the homeless.

The eldest of thirteen brothers and sisters, he was civic minded and delivered meals on wheels into his eighties.

A political activist who loved family and music, but aviation was his life's passion.

Join the Club—Makers, Crafters, Learners, Gardeners

He built toys and loved precision machinery ranging from coffee grinders to German cars and everything in between.

She tried her hand at lepidoptery and mapmaking.

b.1937. A master crafts person, she could sew, embroider, knit, crochet, paint, upholster and decorate like a professional. She worked alongside our father finishing the interior of their house.

Eighty-three years. Experimented with grafting flowers from around the world. Recycled used goods before recycling became fashionable and practical.

He was a creative wood worker. We will remember the cedar strip canoe, beer case storage stands, bird houses, children's games, toys, and doll cribs. Don't forget the wooden salad forks.

She loved all things girly. Her true passions: shopping and knitting.

A woodworker, he created crude pine artifacts. Investing and trading options were hobbies.

Whenever she set her mind to a hobby, she became an expert on it. Over the years her orchids won ribbons, her beloved poodles were champions, and her charming handmade bears were proudly displayed by many people.

He could make anything from knitting sweaters for the entire family, to building homes, stone walls, and furniture. A practical thinker and passionate about the piano.

She had grade five education but was a remarkable woodworker.

She enjoyed all kinds of crafts, particularly card making.

b.1928. She was a stained-glass craftsperson and a taker of courses in everything from comparative theology to pig husbandry.

b.1936. She made Barbie doll clothes and Raggedy Anne and Andy dolls and worked in the fabric department at Eaton's. Later on, she evolved to quilting.

Her artistic skills were expressed most effectively with her Ukrainian egg designs.

Ninety years. She was a member and instructor with an amateur radio club. A life-long interest in camping and a member of a trailer club.

Long-time member of a repeater association.

Japanese flower arranger.

Active member of a clock club, he loved tinkering in his basement with watches and clocks.

An enthusiastic member of the Canadian Celtic choir.

b.1946. President of an optimist club.

A weaver and spinner.

Born in Glasgow, a lifelong model aircraft hobbyist. Member of a remote-control club. A lawn bowler.

Lifetime member of a skating club and a career from high school until retirement with an insurance company.

Her hobbies were sewing and quilting, at which she was meticulous.

b.1925. Style and fashion defined her, and she is remembered for the beautiful creations she wore to the many social events she attended.

Feisty, Stoic, Danced Up a Storm

Full of strong opinions and with curmudgeonly ways.

Recognized for being feisty, opinionated, and enjoying political rants. Cycled and played tennis into her eighties. She could easily beat her daughters at tennis and she danced up a storm to big band music.

b.1948. A member of one of the first gifted classes, he enjoyed reunions with his classmates.

She loved a spirited debate.

He shared his sharp intellect with anyone willing to chat.

His life was colourful and full of excitement.

He was a lucky man, enjoying a fruitful marriage for more than sixty-one years. He lived life on his own terms and rarely complained, a stoic hard worker with a strong sense of fair play. Very little came between him and men's night. He was a fitness buff, running three times a week. He loved his daily Scotch, his winter trips to Sedona and Palm Springs, and a good debate.

Anyone who knew him knew he had an amazing smirk. His motto: why change something if it can be fixed.

Ninety years. He looked forward to new experiences like a young child and leapt at the chance to meet up with old friends. Made hand-made Christmas cards.

An unmatched life, she was tough as nails and the epitome of class. She enjoyed hot weather, red lipstick, and having her hair done.

Known for her feisty spirit, she loved a party and was a champion five-pin bowler.

She never lost her Englishness or her use of English expressions, lost on most Canadians.

Counted on for intelligent, though not unbiased, conversation.

Always gave advice on world affairs.

From humble beginnings, he became a pillar of the community.

b.1965. A lover of all things sparkly, fuzzy or furry, known for her large shoe collection and offbeat sense of humour.

He was always getting around to doing something.

Aiming for a Spot in the After World

At eight, my mum, sister, and I left the suburbs and went to a downtown movie theatre to watch *Old Yeller.* I left the theatre stricken, sobbing for the honourable dog who, having contracted rabies, was shot by the very boy who loved him so. My grief for Old Yeller lasted a long time, although I have no recollection of my older sister crying alongside me and she claims no recollection of having seen the film. It was Old Yeller who opened my interest in the question for which no one can prove the answer: what happens after?

A priest whose brother was also a priest, he became known for his sermons and legendary jazz collection.

She held modern pagan beliefs and took part in covens.

Born in St John's Newfoundland. He fished from the Battery with his grandfather, endured the Depression, and marvelled at radio technology. He studied theology and became a minister in Manitoba, Ontario, and Labrador. He kept cattle and bees.

An active member of her church. Having known hunger and pain, she was dedicated to helping the poor. She had her share of heartaches but grateful for her blessings.

She and her family arrived in Halifax aboard the S.S. Duchess of York in 1934, making their first home in Kirkland Lake. In the early 1940s, she ventured to Ottawa. "I have fought the good fight. I have finished the race, I have kept the faith," ll Timothy 4:7.

The Irish Christian Brothers had the most important spiritual and intellectual influence on him.

Ninety years. Manufactured septic tanks. Born in Germany, he went to Paraguay with a group of Mennonites, then to Canada. A member of the Rosicrucian Order.

He went home to be with the Lord. A wonderful dad who lived his whole life loving the Lord and his family.

She personified the moral guidance of 1 Corinthians 13. She entered the Valley of the Shadow of Death without fear. Her endless suffering has ended. May she rest in peace and her memory spring eternal.

A retired missionary, working for thirty years in Niger, Benin, and Burkina Faso. Raised on a farm on the drought-hardened prairie during the 1930s, as a girl she committed her life to Jesus at an old-fashioned revival meeting.

He served as a friar with the Servants of Mary for forty years throughout Canada

A prayer warrior for many children, missionaries, and friends. High among his many interests was writing Bible tracts. He enjoyed handing out his tract "the Blessings of Canada and Much More" to people.

He went to sleep while watching TV and continued home to be with Jesus. He leaves behind his family, his A.A., and church families.

A reverend, he entered into eternal rest in the Lord. Following graduation from the C.G. Jung institute in Zurich, he established a private practice in analytical psychology.

She made ten pilgrimages to Lourdes.

Homemaker and evangelist for Jesus Christ.

An opera singer and world traveller, she took her final voyage into the arms of her beloved Saviour.

Nuns

My first two girl crushes were nuns. Sister Mary Rose of the Sisters of Charity was my grade-four teacher. She allowed me to stay with her after school and help her mark other students' tests and assignments, clean the chalk board, and tidy up the classroom. The following year, she died young as a result of a surgical complication.

I wanted to be just like Soeur Eugenie de Montfort of the Congregation des Filles de la Sagesse, my second girl crush. She became my piano teacher when I was seven, and I remained her student for seven more years. By that final year, I had lost interest in playing the piano, but Soeur Eugenie was so tenderly caring towards me that I continued on. What I wasn't prepared for was her sudden unannounced relocation to another convent.

Whenever I return to my childhood neighbourhood, I drive slowly along the street where her convent still stands, although it is now a long-term care facility. I look up at the window of the room of my piano lessons, and each time, I feel the same pang of sadness as when I was told that she had left.

She had eleven siblings, and at sixteen, became a nun in order to be a missionary, which she did for sixty years in China and the Dominican Republic. After sixty years, she left the convent.

Sister Mary, a Grey Sister of the Immaculate Conception, twin to Marion, also a Grey Nun.

For thirty years, she was a devoted nun with the Daughters of Wisdom, then she got married.

After retirement as a teacher, she won several ballroom dancing competitions.

She died at age eighty-eight of which sixty-eight were consecrated in religious life.

102 years. Sister of the Holy Cross, she was the only child of her birth parents. Another couple chose her to be their daughter and she became known by a different surname.

A nun for nine years, later she married.

A member of the Daughters of Wisdom, she was called to teach to deaf and blind children in Colombia. Also taught in Madrid and was a missionary in New Guinea.

Chapter 5

A Death in the Family

First of all learn about death, and then about other things.
—Nicherin Daishonin

In the mornings, we kids made heads from clay the size of grapefruits that shifted wet at the shoreline in front of the family cottage. Each head with eyes, mouth, nose, ears, no neck. We left the heads to dry on the edge of the wharf during the day before lacquering them to present to parents, aunts, and uncles. If though, an exuberant friend—and it was mostly Diana who, to our constant irritation always walked on her toes—bounced on to the wharf, a head could easily topple into the water. Once there, it either dissolved into a gooey mass swirling the water beige to blond, or if it had been left on the wharf until mid-afternoon, the disembodied head cracked into pieces. Either way, the head was gone. Gone now are Diana and two other friends who created the clay heads with me. Gone too are the parents, the aunts, the uncles. Even the shoreline has become something else.

When a Mother Dies

In 1983, my mother's obituary was written by the funeral home director. It provided date of birth and death, names of her family members, where and when her funeral will take place. There was neither a picture of her nor a description of her life. Leading the service was a minister who had never met her and who omitted to mention that she had two living sisters and a brother, all three sitting in the front row.

It's a sad time for all of us, but our mum would say "Don't worry, it'll happen to us all in the end." Bon voyage.

She was Mum, not just to her own motley crew, but to all the kids who knew her. She grew up in Saskatchewan during the Great Depression and through her Prairie upbringing, she learned to approach challenges with common sense. Unfailingly polite and a backbone of steel in matters of principle. She gave her four sons individual, initialed lunches (the envy of other students). There was a parade of neighbourhood kids in and around the house, even though she often finished reading a book in one day. A strong female role model for her daughters-in-law and granddaughter. She showed what true feminism means.

She will be greatly missed by her dearest friend, Margaret, and also her daughter and her sister.

Passed away peacefully of a broken heart. Please join us to say goodbye to our mom.

A loving mother, she will be fondly remembered by her stepdaughters.

Mum will always be remembered as a woman with unmeasurable strength just like her mum. Donation to a violence against women program of your choosing.

Yes, some women do have five boys and no girls, and some have six girls and no boys. The first is my mum and the second is her sister. All of us are now motherless.

Raised on a farm at Sweet's Corners, Ontario, she learned how to handle draft horses, wrangle a dairy herd using a switch from a willow tree, make the best raspberry pie ever tasted, plant a vegetable garden, and care for others. Married in an evening ceremony that was resplendent with flowers grown on her family farm, they raised a family of three while she maintained her nursing career. After her children left home, she became a skilled machine knitter. She taught herself to sail and earned her pilot's licence. She continued on with her thirty-six-year career as a soprano and soloist in her church choir and was a critic of the latest Murdoch Mysteries episodes. She was the chief listener. She was the best listener.

She leaves behind her four daughters who were her estranged children. She is finally at peace.

When planning her family, she decided that three children would be best so that she would have the necessary number for playing Bridge. We felt obliged to comply: resistance was futile. A perfectionist, organized, political, a bibliophile, logophile (go google that), creative baker, hostess, teacher, manager, gardener, volunteer, internet researcher, editor, humorous, sharp-witted, multi-lingual, Virgo, fashionable, a debater, animal lover, loyal, rational, analytical, hard worker, practical, problem solver, activist, scrabbler, knitter, and seamstress.

She died a month after losing her son.

Being a single mother in the 1960s was not easy.

She was devoted to her family with no consideration for herself. She loved caring for her family.

Predeceased by her infant daughter and her granddaughter.

Predeceased by both her children.

She leaves behind her son, the apple of her eye.

She lost her two children to cystic fibrosis and her husband at an early age.

Cherished mommy to her two children.

Leaves behind her children and her great grandson.

She was a dedicated wife of fifty-two years, always making herself available to anyone needing her help. She supported many Christian missions and children's orphanages throughout her lifetime and sacrificed her own career to focus on her family. She will be remembered for her ability to help others.

As a single parent, a widow, she nurtured and raised her son and was a constant influence in the formation of his moral and ethical compass and drive.

She had five kids in six years. Later in life, she liked to hike on her own.

Despite challenges, she managed to create and sustain a strong, loving family and remain full of life herself. She had strength beyond comprehension and the patience of Job. Her family's rock, lighthouse, and greatest source of comfort, understanding and unconditional love.

She had forty-three happy years of marriage and raised four mischievous boys. They had an incredible ride. Survived by her husband, sons, and stepdaughters.

b.1961. Her grandchildren were her reasons for not giving up without a heroic fight.

She loved a quick visit to the casino or a few hours playing cards. She was the glue that kept the family circus organized and focussed. Proud of her Irish heritage (County Kilkenny), she will be with us in enthusiastic spirit each St. Patrick's Day.

After many years as a stay-at-home mum, she bravely went back to school and became a teacher. Survived by her granddaughter and sister-in-law.

She gave up her driver's licence at 101. When asked why she would need her licence at 100, she replied to go to the drug store, the library, church, and the liquor store.

The youngest of three girls born near a small hamlet in Southeast Saskatchewan. She was raised on the family farm and attended school, walking or riding in a cart pulled by a Shetland pony. After marriage, they borrowed money to build their first home and got as far as completing the foundation when she found out she was pregnant. They sold the unfinished house and her husband re-enlisted in the Air Force requiring him to leave her to await her baby's birth. In 1954, he was diagnosed with tuberculosis, contracted while they were in Northern British Columbia, and had to enter a sanatorium for treatment, making it necessary for her to take her new baby and toddler to live with her parents on the farm for a year while he recovered.

Queer Family Members

Until the midpoint of the twentieth century, British obituary writers employed the phrase "he never married" as code indicating the deceased was gay. From time to time, it was also descriptive of an unmarried straight man. That a family member was queer remains infrequently mentioned in obituaries.

Only twenty-two, he is survived by his boyfriend.

b.1961. A devotee of disco music, fondly remembered for his thoughtful ruminations on politics and issues related to the LGBTQ community. A committed social activist particularly focused on gay rights, accessibility, and mental health.

Frank, beloved husband of Bill.

She is survived by her partner, Rose, of fifty years.

b.1928. He will join Andrew, partner of 70 years. He collected exotic carpets, antique furniture, and loved the indigenous cultures of Mexico and South America.

Cancer wins again so it thought. It may have her body but not her spirit. Survived by her wife, her son and daughter.

In later life, he volunteered with an AIDS organization and a project supporting LGBTQ refugees.

He leaves behind his husband. They had a great love of twenty-five years filled with travel, friendships, and entertaining. He had two children with his first spouse.

Tell me, what is it you plan to do
With your one wild and precious life.
—Mary Oliver, *The Summer Day*

When a Sibling Dies

Serving as a historical document, a truncated biography, a social commentary on the times, each obituary heralds a new personal world order for family members and friends. Obits reveal a family's circumstances, power differentials, complexity of relationships, the strengths and weaknesses of emotional bonds, and siblings' ties to one another.

She burned up the phone lines with her big brother.

Her lifelong partner in adventure, best friend, and brother, she will find his loss irreplaceable.

The second of five girls who were orphaned at a young age and raised at a convent school. As a result, she was devoted to her sisters.

His own man, a blue baby at birth, he came into this world struggling—a theme that followed him throughout his life. He faced the challenges that were foisted on him and never agreed with how the world worked. He despised pretense. He saw his mistakes and regretted the important ones. He would have been happy surrounded by nature and listening to BB King. Although I'm the college graduate and the older brother, he's the one who had key insights into the world. He accepted me as I am well before I could accept myself. You will always be my biggest supporter and my best friend. We are all forever changed for the better by your twisted sense of humour.

Married in a double ceremony with her sister.

Our beautiful sister died, although alcoholism had taken her soul from us much earlier. We will always know her as our kind and luminous sister.

At ten, her parents died and she and her sister left Winnipeg to live with relatives. She spent many hours playing cards.

He was the fourth born child and always maintained he was the favourite, but that is still unclear and thus the final ruling must be litigated in family court or at a bar. He loved his children and grandchildren, but what followed as a very close second was his love for the Blue Jays. He had a unique bag of one liners.

Survived by five siblings.

An idyllic childhood and winner of several ballroom dance competitions with his sister.

The eighth of nine children, both of her parents died when she was two. She never married.

Naming the Adoptees, the Adopters, the Stepchildren

The adoption document states that Renata, just over two, and her brother Gilberto, just under one, were fed by neighbours for a short period of time until they could no longer feed them and they were then left on a sidewalk. An unknown person took them to a nearby police station.

The document further indicates that Maria, their birth mother, lives, or perhaps now lived in Sao Paulo, Brazil. By the time Renata and Gilberto were brought to the police station, Maria's two older children, Alessandra and Alex, were in separate orphanages and had been for several years. The document mentions that Maria's life is, or perhaps was, coloured by extreme poverty. It notes that she had a long scar across her face, that she lived in one room without windows, and that she was affective toward Renata and Gilberto. They were placed in different orphanages.

There is no further information concerning Maria. Not her date of birth or what she looked like or what she liked. Or if she wails for her children, all living in another country, speaking a language she doesn't understand, nor would they now understand hers. Or if her heart holds heavy in the missing and yearning for her children, not knowing where they are, how they are, not knowing them any longer.

If Maria no longer lives, and if she had had an obit, would it state, "Bereft mother of Alex, Alessandra, Renata, and Gilberto, she spent much of her life grieving for her children gone from her"?

The human condition assures us of that not all life stories fit neatly into obits.

Some people fill in crossword puzzles. I read obits. Every day. I read —stepson, adopted daughter, the ranking of children. I read—father of Joan and Paul and adopted son, Simon. I read—mother of Katie, Frank, and stepdaughter, Paula. The need to categorize, to define belonging, degrees of closeness and distance, the need to state that the relationship was created other than through birth ties.

Obits' most emphasized feature of a deceased person's life is who they loved and who loved them. Whether a partner, parents, children, friends, or pets, rarely is a life described without love. But families are also spaces of hierarchy and obits evidence this. Levels of love, of belonging, endure. Obits show much about a family's structure, about children, about estrangement, about how those who had adopted, how those who had been adopted, and how those who were stepchildren, fit. In the listing of those mentioned by closeness to the deceased, stepchildren and adopted children can be placed following aunts, uncles, and friends, while birth children rank following partner and at times before the partner.

When Renata came to Canada, she was four. Two days later, we shopped for clothing for her. Although first time in a mall, first time in a children's clothing store, she innately possessed a particular sense of style. Clear about what she liked, the design, the colours, what and how to accessorize, she picked out a tiny shimmering purple over-the-shoulder purse, which remained with her for years. In her orphanage, clothes were selected for her from large general bins. On our shopping day she wholeheartedly selected. A few years later, her sense of flair further emerged: she sewed her own clothes, blocking colours for the look she wanted. For me, she created vests and housecoats.

Renata has her own child now, Silvio. His name: "the boy from the forest." He is contented, comfortable. My daughters' ancestors were taken from Africa to Brazil, his life unimagined by them. He has three grandmothers, each in a separate continent. One, Maria, Renata's birth mother, is alive or not in Brazil. Does Maria wonder if she might be a grandmother?

The best surprise of my life was the reunion with my son, who I gave up for adoption many years ago and who recently called my brother in British Columbia.

Predeceased by her birth parents and her adoptive parent.

Adopted at three, she was fortunate to later find her birth mother and had a happy but sadly short relationship with her as she lost her soon after.

To her death, she maintained a happy relationship with her birth mother's and birth father's family.

Raised by his adoptive parents.

The adopted daughter of her parents.

She had good relations with her birth father's family. Some members visited her just days before her death.

Predeceased by his father, his son, stepbrothers, and stepsister.

Lovingly raised by his grandparents.

Remembered by her sister, grandparents, and adopted sister.

Death of a Father

During the visitation prior to my father's funeral, my sister and I walk together towards his open casket, aware of others noticing as we stand there. We whisper to each other. One of us points to the crease on our father's nose between his eyes. The other says "I have the same line." For some reason we start laughing, and in our attempts to suppress this, we both bend over the casket. Our backs shake as we become giddier. My sister stands and races towards a side door. I follow. It leads us outside where we continue to laugh until a cousin, concerned for us, comes our way and we return inside.

b.1930. Our father was born in the worst decade of the century—a time when grown men rode the rails looking for work and begging for scraps at back door stoops. It was a world where a little boy lost his mother and sister to diseases easily curable today and where his older brother went to war not knowing if he would return.

Born on a warm, sunny day, at eight he developed a lifelong interest in electronics by reading his uncle Mel's Popular Mechanics magazines. He loved amateur radio, fixing broken mechanical equipment and electronics, and feeding squirrels.

He died only weeks after the passing of his loved daughter.

Predeceased by his first wife. Survived by his second wife, Jane, his sister Constance, and his stepchildren.

Our patriarch has concluded his lifetime story.

His first wife predeceased him, and we are thankful that he recently reconnected with their two children.

Left to grieve, his children, his former wife and her husband, and his common-law partner.

He took care of us for one hundred and four and a half years.

Eternally saddened by the untimely loss of three of his six children.

Fondly remembered by the children who he assisted in raising. Survived by his wife.

He loved our son unconditionally.

The most difficult part of his life was the loss of his daughter at the age of fifteen.

He couldn't wait to show his children how the world worked.

He ran hot and cold. He could be full of love or full of anger. Compassionate or harsh. We knew when to give him a wide berth. He would often pick up the tab. He was frequently in trouble as a teen.

Predeceased by his wife, he leaves his grandchildren to mourn.

Died with her husband of seventy-four years by her side. One month later, her husband died.

The night before he died, he watched It's a Wonderful Life with his family.

Dad went looking for mum on date night and found her. He would drop off bags of groceries for his tenants when he knew they were going through tough times. He taught his daughter to always save for a rainy day and to pay attention when people show their true colours.

He called us kids by each others' names. He never wished us a happy birthday on the right day.

Son of an English coal miner.

A Partner's Death

Died suddenly, five days before his wedding day. Donations can be made to True Patriot Love Foundation, which supports wounded vets, a cause dear to his heart.

Luck smiled on her when she reconnected with her high school sweetheart. The two were inseparable from that moment on.

She met him on a blind date and they probably never imagined they'd be together sixty-five years later.

Predeceased by her two loving husbands.

Sixty-three years of faithful marriage to the love of his life. Remembered for his gentleness, patience, servant's heart, and powerful handshake.

She passed from a broken heart shortly after her husband died.

She eloped with a handsome man.

After just one date, he foretold he would marry his wife.

He married his soul mate in his fifties, and they planned to move to their dream home but for his sudden death.

She met her husband on campus, and when he saw her, he simply thought, there she is.

She went with her beloved husband curled up beside her as she took her final breath.

He leaves his wife and his former wife. As per his wishes, there will be no funeral.

Born on the Ides of March while his father was fighting in WW2. His parents fought often and with intensity. He was a proud founder of a bottle club. He met his future wife at a party while on a date with another girl. They had four children and built a cottage by a lake. In spite of a divorce and several long-term partners, she was the love of his life, something he never let her forget. Larger than life, charming, quick-witted, quirky, sentimental, loyal, outspoken—he was a showman.

She had an "interesting" marriage with her husband. They were very different from each other.

He and his wife fostered more than one hundred babies.

A three-time widow, and after that, she was with another man.

He died on his fiftieth wedding anniversary.

After a long life together, they died one day apart.

They were devoted lovers and dear friends.

He died while swimming and in the arms of his wife with whom he reconnected after forty years.

He left us in his sleep one week following the tragic loss of his darling wife. He was not prepared to go on without her, yet he wasn't prepared to leave her while she was on this earth.

His marriage was the stuff of 1950s movies, the handsome football quarterback marrying the beauty queen. But beneath the surface was a man who wrestled with demons.

Now together forever. They died within a few hours of each other, neither ever knowing that the other was gone. It was a perfect ending to a beautiful life-long love affair, a fairy tale romance from their first dance during the war in 1941.

Announcing a Child's Death

A child's death alters the world for their family. How a child dies, the difficulty to stand in the belief of it, the awareness of it, forces the breath to tighten, and the hard ball of pain in the chest, the heart, the neck, brings home the truth of this death.

How does a mother write an obit for her six-year-old daughter or her fourteen-year-old son? Rather than looking forward, she is forced to look back and resist an urge to focus on what won't be.

b.1992. He suffered an aneurysm after a day well-lived. He was our fourth and final baby, the one who completed our family. His roommate's valiant efforts of resuscitation won't be forgotten.

She was happy to have been the cherished daughter of her parents.

He enjoyed the help of countless support workers at home and at school.

Predeceased by his mother and his estranged father.

Raised by his grandmother and aunt. He loved the Sens hockey team and took part in a day program for children with special needs.

When an Infant Dies

One day old. No words can describe our heartbreak, our broken hearts. We've never felt agony like this before.

Died at ten days old.

She was predeceased by her infant twins.

We said goodbye to our precious baby.

We take comfort in the knowledge that she is now with her grandfather and grandmother.

People forget years and remember moments.
—Ann Beattie, novelist

Picturing the Deceased

Even as a toddler, I cringed when I've had my photo taken. At three, I refused to pose for a professional photo of myself and my calmer sister, older than me by two years. I fidgeted and cried. The selected picture shows my more compliant sister smiling, her wee fingers crossed through each other with me beside her bearing an expression of fatigue within an odd almost semi-smile. The adults, too, were spent by then.

The task of selecting which photo to present a life, the chosen one hopefully encapsulating a feature, or the essence, the truth of a person. An uncommon decision.

The photo of the middle-aged man holding high a large fish he had just caught was the first one that grabbed my attention. Since then, my attention has been held by a cheerful father wearing a hardhat, a woman bald from chemotherapy, a carefree looking young man smoking a cigarette, another looking to the side with a cigar in his mouth, an adolescent ill in a bed, a mother in a wheelchair, an eighty-year-old man smiling in a bathtub.

A person beside a pool on a cruise ship. A middle-aged man leaning cockily against a cool car, an older man on his tractor in a field. A woman with a granddaughter in her arms, another woman with a large glass of bubbly, a cottage setting behind her. A woman seemingly enjoying a meal in a long-term care facility cafeteria. The just-married thirty years ago, bride and groom smiling to the camera, to the future.

Many obits include a single photo, some include two—the younger self and the matured version. Some return to a person's childhood, identifiable now only by a parent, sibling, or long-time friend. Photos from a long-departed adolescence highlight a high school graduation or a prom twenty-five years before. A few show a young man on a motorcycle or a young woman on a towel at a beach.

A person sits in a rocking or garden chair alongside a dog, or with a cat sleeping on their lap. Once in a while, a person stands beside a goat, a cow, a horse, the animal named in the obit.

People in identifying work uniforms abound. We look at nurses with their white dresses and starched caps of the past, stalwart RCMP officers, paramedics, and firefighters photo ready in their uniforms.

Not all photos show a happy person. Some appear serious, or dampened in expression, or belligerent, grumpy, or plainly straightforward. They're all there in the obits.

Those with the shortest lives, the newborns, are swaddled in a blanket, small cap on their heads, eyes closed.

Family Pets

Toady, my small turtle, died two months after my mother brought her home for me from a pet store. I was five and I responded to her death with disbelief. Don't cry, I was told. It's just a turtle. I wanted to know more and with the news from my parents that they had buried her, I was relieved. Years later, I found that Toady had never received that burial.

As a young girl I wanted a dog. Toady the turtle was my first dog replacement, followed by Peewee, the Mediterranean blue budgie. Neither worked out well. The following Christmas, my parents promised me a dog and yes, I did receive a dog—a tiny child's toy on wheels, a grey schnauzer with a skinny red plastic leash and a name tag around her neck, Tessa. My father laughed when he confirmed that my wish had come true. My mother didn't speak. (Growing up, her family had dogs, and one that she particularly liked, Tony the fox terrier).

It wasn't until I turned thirty that I spotted the sole dog at the Humane Society who didn't come to the front of her cage when I entered the cacophonous room—the other dogs desperate for attention, but not her, overtaken by fear. Puppy, renamed Poppy the collie, came home with me.

Since then, with each dog I've lived with, I've loved the most recent the most. Or perhaps I continue to learn about their wonderfulness and appreciate how they spread their love at my feet, on my lap, stretched on a couch, running in a field, how they know how to suggest a special culinary item just right for them. How each one has known my expressions of joy, frustration, sadness, how each one comforted and was comforted, how they learned my words, my habits, my cues, and how they knew and touched my soul.

Unless your pet is an African grey parrot or macaw, you might live longer than them and I've outlived several dogs. When each one died, I grieved and believed it too hard to live with another. But I always have, their kind-heartedness drawing me back. With each, I grow in awareness of how they love being alive and how much is taken away by their death. Which, if any of the photos of my dogs walking with me in the woods or standing beside would I select for my obit? The pictured telling of one feature from a whole life. I prefer it to be of me without a dog, and recent, and semi-smiling.

My current dog, Bobby, is now elderly. I have more grieving to do.

They raised their sons and showed their dogs.

Her precious dog, Babe, comforted her on her journey dying.

He was known when walking around town as the old man with the nice-looking dog.

He was predeceased by his dog. Yes, he would want you to know that.

A breeder of Dandie Dinmonts and some were prize winners.

He had a special fondness for Chihuahua puppies.

His favourite pal, Happy, is waiting to welcome him to Heaven.

Missed by her little man, Pancho.

He leaves to mourn the friends he met on the dog trails with his best friend Maisie.

His dog, Paddy, is patiently waiting for his next walk with him.

Preceded in death by her cats.

She will be missed by her horse.

She loved exotic pets and fish.

Her home was filled with animals—guinea pigs, snakes, monkeys.

b.1960. He opened his house to people and animals in need. He took in dogs and cats and orphaned squirrels. And had a love hate relationship with raccoons.

Created new varieties of daylilies. Showed miniature schnauzers.

His love of thoroughbred horse racing was well known.

He leaves behind his little buddy, Buddy.

Passed away with his faithful dog, Max, by his side.

Some of his favourite times were spent flipping burgers for Canada Day celebrations and exercising his green thumb. He had an endearing fondness for his four-legged friend Casey, who provided him with much comfort.

His dog, Valentine, will miss him.

May she be at peace with her beloved dog, Lassie.

Donations to Courageous Champions, a charity providing service dogs to military veterans and first responders with physical and/or psychological injuries.

As dad loved a good pup, donations to an animal shelter would make him smile.

We ask that you kindly make a donation to a cat sanctuary, a charity that was dear to his heart.

Donations: Guide Dogs for the Blind Association.

Donations to a Pomeranian and small breed rescue in honour of her

Chapter 6

Talk about Health

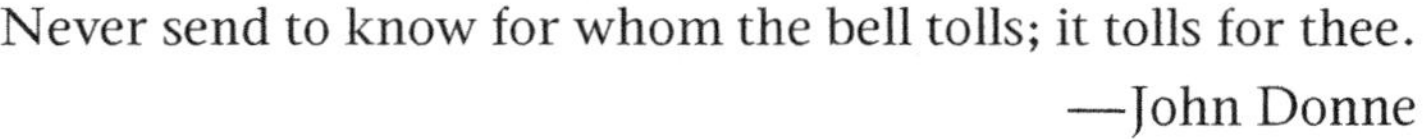

Never send to know for whom the bell tolls; it tolls for thee.
—John Donne

A big heart and a stubborn streak to match. It helped her to get through many years of pain. She is now free to run, skip, or walk.

Well, it appears the brain tumour has won.

He defied medical predictions and survived in relative comfort well beyond his best before date.

Born without vital signs and surviving sepsis three times, she lived until ninety-two.

He diligently pursued alternative treatments in a number of countries around the world.

With profound shock we announce that although she faced many challenges in her short life, she met each with resolve.

Injured at nine resulting in paraplegia, he participated in wheelchair sports, especially basketball, tennis, and table tennis.

Despite ill health, he frequently expressed his gratitude for his fulsome life with family and friends. Always up for a challenge.

After a long battle with AIDS. He watched most of his friends pass away in the 1980s from AIDS and was told his death would be within a few months. He lived more than another thirty years with the help of many people, including his doctors.

Sixty-seven years. He struggled with his health, often with one complication leading to another. In the end it was his brave heart that gave. The bottom line is that his pain is no more.

Peacefully, after battling MS for over thirty years, at the age of fifty-one.

She was born with Down syndrome and against the advice of doctors to institutionalize her, they brought her home to give her the best upbringing. And thrive she did. In her early twenties, she moved to a L'Arche home and loved it there.

She worked hard in her life to control her type 1 diabetes, acquired at age ten.

With grace, despite the medical challenges that faced him.

b.1954. ALS claims another life too soon. He climbed the ladder from bag boy to regional director of his grocery chain. No one could stump him with any classic car question.

After a doomed battle with Huntington's disease.

Born with Down syndrome, his life trajectory was formed by a wise doctor who said that all babies need lots of love. He was denied access to school until he was sixteen, and even then, it was in a segregated school.

Two weeks after falling and breaking a hip.

Fifty-two years. She lived her life to the fullest as if tomorrow would never come. She knew she was living on borrowed time but never gave it a second thought. She refused to let her challenges defeat her.

Giving Organs, Receiving Organs

He did not have the strength to leave his brother's home to attend his mother's ninetieth birthday party, so the party was brought to him. He was hoping for a second liver transplant when he died.

A generous organ donor.

For the fifty years since his birth, he endured illness, kidney transplants, years of teasing and bullying, but he never complained, never asked, or expected any favours. He beat the odds until he got cancer. Now he is pain free.

b.1943. Thank you to the unknown donor family for giving him ten years post–liver transplant.

b.1948. He was given a second chance at life when he received a double lung transplant two years ago.

> When people die, they cannot be replaced. They leave holes that cannot be filled, for it is the fate—the genetic and neural fate—of every human being to be a unique individual, to find his own path, to live his own life, to die his own death.
>
> —Dr. Oliver Sacks

Emotional Challenges

My daughter, Alessandra, spent five of her early years in an orphanage, a place with little protection. Professionals classify the type of events she experienced there as adverse childhood experiences (ACEs). They list and categorize each ACE and the resultant harm it exposes a child to. Alessandra experienced emotional damages that were never entirely undone.

Obits of those suffering from emotional trauma or mental illness interplay the years of struggles, emotional pain, the description of the person as both with the illness and apart from it, and the desire to right society's treatment of those with mental illness. The person, the illness, and the request to see beyond the illness are laid out. These people are often young.

We mourn the sudden loss of a humble and gentle young man who could no longer battle his mental illness and is now at eternal peace. Those who had the fortune to know him will forever remember his gentle soul. He impacted the lives of others through his kindness and sensitivity.

He struggled with darkness.

Our mental health system has failed too many people, and his dying wish was to bring awareness to mental illness. He had an artist's soul and was well known for his work as a body modification artist.

The demons will no longer be with her.

A magic trickster, origamist, yoyoer, gamer, cinephile, melophile, epicure, dreamer, inventor, tragic figure. System victim. Please donate to bipolar research, Canadian Mental Health Association.

He lived life to extremes, neither moderate nor boring. He was generous to a fault.

He fought an uphill battle with mental illness since his teenage years.

She grappled with bipolar illness and depression. She visited places she never thought a farm girl could go to.

He struggled a long time with mental illness and addiction. Say a prayer for those still suffering from alcoholism.

b.1987. His creative talent was in the composition of beautiful music, and he played the guitar for many hours a day even as a young boy. He made music the biggest focus of his existence. He rendered his photographs in his dark room. He saw light but he also struggled with darkness like many creative people. His cat Henry was worshipped and hugged. He will be excruciatingly missed. Please donate to a homeless shelter.

Suffering from schizoaffective disorder, he walked to the beat of a different drum all his life. His emotional and thought disorder caused him much suffering during his life, but his gift for conversation made him a delightful companion.

Just shy of his twenty-first birthday. Donation to a mental health hospital please.

After a long and difficult journey with her mental health, she died at twenty-three. Appreciating the importance of creating an awareness and dialogue around mental health, she spoke about it bravely and beautifully.

She was seventeen and fought against depression and substance abuse.

He was so young. Please donate to the Children's Hospital mental health program.

He died suddenly at home at twenty-two years. Please donate to the Mental Health Foundation.

Twenty-six years old, he struggled many years with schizophrenia and managed, with great courage, to have the best possible life he could.

She was taken tragically from her younger sisters. If you know someone who is struggling, reach out. Everyone has value.

He knew the depths of depression and battled with it, finally finding sobriety and spiritual reading. He had a sense of humour.

She had a holistic and spiritual approach to life and loved yoga and meditation. Donations to a mental health hospital.

He struggled with the burden of depression. His inspirations included Voltaire, Thomas Jefferson, Frederic Bastiat, Eckhart Tolle, Roger Waters, and Ron Paul. He loved nature, meditation, and yoga. Please donate to depression research.

She was a sociable person, yet she struggled with profound mental illness and spent thirty years in and out of mental institutions.

On a beautiful Sunday morning, after breakfast, our brother went to Heaven to see dad, whom he had missed for years. His ashes will be buried next to his younger brother. He volunteered tirelessly with the group, Psychiatric Survivors. He lived bravely with mental illness for most of his adult life. Rest in the arms of God.

His brain injury affected his mental health. He died at twenty-six.

Pointing Directly to Suicide

This lovely soul passed away at his home, tragically taking his own life. Donations to Canadian Association for Suicide Prevention.

He died by suicide after a bitter battle with depression.

A soldier, he lost the battle against PTSD.

Cancer

After an unchoreographed dance with breast cancer, she initially took the lead, but the rapid dips and slides became too much after eighteen months.

He had cancer three times but lost the war when the toll on his heart became too great.

He died too soon, felled by a relentless cancer.

She fought a good battle with cancer. After a year, she died peacefully having endured a ravaging and incurable cancer.

Surrendered to a brave battle with cancer.

Dementia

He lived with a partner called Alzheimer's.

Died after a month in hospital where she was distraught from Alzheimer's. To those who knew her, those difficulties contrasted with her life filled with affection and happiness. Being an only daughter and demonstrating an eagerness to learn, her parents provided her with lessons in music, dancing, and skating, which progressed to travel for competitions and concerts. She continued weekly tennis, badminton, and hiking until her early eighties. Her English mother, a war bride, ingrained in her Victorian attitudes of manner and dress, which served her well all her life. She enjoyed escapades of parasailing and submarining, and camel, oxen, elephant, and donkey rides. During her eightieth birthday, the family was enjoined to forget the words parachuting or bungee jumping and the day was saved when her son-in-law took her for a motorcycle ride.

Like her mother, she spent the last decades of her life with Alzheimer's.

Sadly, we began mourning him a few years ago, when he was diagnosed with dementia. As the disease progressed, he was slowly taken from us. In spite of his love of children, he was unable to enjoy his grandchildren as we know he would have liked.

No more suffering, no more pain, no more Alzheimer's disease.

Chapter 7

The Meaning of Work

Matter is never lost
I eat the fruit of the tree
You are buried beneath.
—Christina Tang-Bernas

Not all nurses marry doctors, and not all nurses get married. Obits highlight careers and work. Some people loved their work and proudly achieved success as they scrambled ahead, their work their life's accomplishment. Others remained indifferent to their work life and just kept on. Some not even that. And others were employed in hazardous jobs. He died while working at a construction site.

Women at Work

The seventh child of a large farming family, she was nothing short of a firecracker. She pioneered working outside the home for a generation of women. Unexpectedly a single mother to a young family of five, she operated a Voyageur Bus Terminal for fifty years. She knew how to get rid of "hooey" and what to say to lighten the mood or get her point across, whichever could be deemed most needed in the moment.

She beat out eight men on the civil service exams. They all went on to become deputy ministers.

Born on a farm in 1929, she worked at the Canadian Bank Note at a time when few women held down jobs outside the home. She worked there until her marriage when it was no longer acceptable for a woman to work. She worked tirelessly beside her husband on their farm. A snowmobiler, most weekends you could find them heading out in their trailer.

104 years. The matriarch. She was the first female supervisor at her company and mentor to many young women. An athlete, a caregiver for her parents until they died, the no-nonsense yet kind pillar of our family. She enjoyed Chinese food, sherry, fashion, a good joke, and people, especially children most of all.

Having immigrated from Ukraine to a Manitoba farm, she spent the Depression operating her own trap lines to supplement the family income.

b.1927. She excelled in math and won a scholarship to Cambridge University. Until 1948, women graduates were only granted a title to a university degree. In 1998, she and other women of her era were invited back to Cambridge to officially graduate and take their rightful place beside men in a historical graduation ceremony that granted them the full rights and privileges to the Cambridge University degree. An extremely proud moment in her life.

One of the first six women accepted in the Bachelor of Commerce program at her university.

Born into a working-class family in a village in France. Due to hard work and a keen intellect, she earned scholarships through to the time she received her Doctor of Medicine degree.

She left family hardship in Saskatchewan at fifteen to live with relatives. She sewed as a thrifty habit for her kids, but it grew and she became a master seamstress, making wedding dresses and adaptations for folks with special needs.

She was one of the only twenty-six women who graduated in law at McGill University in all the 1940s and 50s.

In the Fields

Particular professions are highlighted in obits as well as the characteristics of those involved in these professions. Farmers described as happy. Teachers dedicated and proud. Professors read as curious people. We are told that some accountants are passionate about their work. At times, a particular work ethic, important to that person, is specified.

A long-time beef farmer, his first love was farming. If you knew him, you understood his appreciation for old-time country music.

He worked hard on the family farm all his life and developed mechanical skills as befitting a farmer. Lived a full but simple life and had no complaints. A man of few words, quiet, always willing to help a neighbour.

She and her husband had a farm of black angus cattle. She helped bring in the hay while wearing high-heeled shoes with her jeans. When her husband died, she and her husband's brother remained good friends. The friendship blossomed and they married.

At thirteen, he ran a farm singlehandedly in Manitoba after the death of his uncle.

A farmer all his life, he tended to his cattle and his beloved dogs. He enjoyed going to local auction sales and always came home with a box of trinkets. He could be found down in his workshop, working on one of his many projects. Gone to be with his family and friends.

He spent his days farming and driving trucks. His favourite saying: "Don't worry, be happy." And that was how he lived his life, randomly bursting into song.

A hard-working farmer, he operated both a dairy and cash crop business. Had a wicked sense of humour and sharp mind.

The second youngest of twelve children, he was raised on a farm in Cobourg, Ontario. He loved the farming life and all that it entailed. He never returned to classes until after the fall harvest.

After a career as a medical doctor, he achieved his lifelong goal of owning a farm.

He ran a chicken farm and was a teacher, then principal.

A truck driver for thirty years and always a proud farmer.

A carpenter, but in retirement, he became a happy farmer.

A farmer all his life, he wanted fiddle music playing as he was dying.

A lifetime dairy farmer.

Fondly remembered by many as a farmer at heart.

In the Classroom

At nineteen, she started teaching in a two-room schoolhouse. A mentor to young girls in Canadian Girls in Training (CGIT).

A lifelong learner and valedictorian of her high school, she earned several scholarships and was one of only three women accepted into the pre-med program at Queen's University. She instead completed a languages degree and taught in a one-room country school until she married. She read biographies and autobiographies and had eight children.

The skills learned in the military led him to teaching and he enjoyed a long-career correcting math exams and patrolling the halls of various high schools.

Much of her life was spent as a primary school teacher shaping young minds.

An old-fashioned shop teacher.

She was a teacher at a Catholic school, even though she was a Protestant. After three dates, she and her husband were married.

He demonstrated a talent for mathematics at a young age and turned that into a life committed to education.

He took great pride in his teaching career.

A high school teacher whose summers were spent shining up his toys: cars, a truck, and boats.

A popular schoolteacher for decades, she was known for going beyond the call of duty to care for those who could benefit from her guidance and upbeat, playful presence.

He taught hairdressing at the local college.

During his entire schooling, his father was his only teacher in a one-room schoolhouse.

Her passion for literacy was demonstrated by her dedicated teaching of English reading skills for new Canadians. She became involved in many civic issues and charitable causes.

In the Lab

Devoted a large part of his academic career to advancing a greater understanding of the works of Thomas Aquinas, questioning whether Aquinas had succeeded in demonstrating the existence of angels and examining the relationship between body and soul. He approached death with acceptance and curiosity. He lived without pretence.

He wanted to be remembered for his teaching and scholarship in Greek.

A music professor who created a legacy of talent that will live on. Many of her students have gone on to successful professional careers in music.

A renowned mathematician, he inspired thousands of students with his simple yet eloquent teaching style. He worked alongside brilliant colleagues.

PhD in medieval studies and grateful for those who helped him and his family immigrate to Canada under difficult political circumstances. He honoured them by helping others do the same.

Behind the screen of the ordinary can be
found unique and wonderful things.
—Ted Kooser

Working Hard and Succeeding Mightily, Sometimes

Tom, my father, was outspoken, handsome, and a guy who "shot from the hip." An extrovert and someone who today we would call old-school, he started out in a rough part of Glasgow. Working in a mine as a young teenager, he hard scrabbled his way from Scotland to Montreal, where in his twenties, he organized Saturday night dances. He became a convincing salesperson, sales manager, then made his way to vice-presidency of a mid-size company. He lived with high stress at his job, partly his personality, partly the type of work, until a heart attack forced his earlier than wanted retirement.

An exceptional mason, he was one of the winners of the Consumers' Choice Award in the category of chimney construction and services.

He had a tremendously successful lunch counter at a shopping centre. He employed numerous new Canadian immigrants.

She worked diligently promoting excellence in customer service at the bank for thirty years.

At twenty-four, he began building his successful life insurance business.

A proud member of Canada's foreign service. Served with unparalleled dedication to task, to fact, to truth, and to the Canadian people.

Even in childhood he was an entrepreneur, raising and selling chickens and their eggs door-to-door along with magazine subscriptions. By age nineteen he operated Christmas tree lots while publishing ad-filled desk blotters for university students.

In her early fifties, she graduated from grade twelve and started a successful bakery.

She grew up an outdoors girl, riding horses at the family farm and hunting with her father. One evening when dad said, "You look like the cat that's eaten the canary," she replied, "Well, I got a job today!" She excelled in her new position in women's retail. She loved the challenge and the camaraderie. Nothing was impossible. Drapes became evening gowns, pinecones became picture frames. Her determination and ingenuity with a screwdriver, a sewing machine, or a pool vacuum are infamous within the family.

Following his apprenticeship in the Glasgow shipbuilding yards, he was awarded admission to the engineering program at Strathclyde University.

A well-respected businessman in the financial world. Throughout his illustrious career he found great success.

A salesman to look up to.

A successful career with Revenue Canada.

Despite an extremely modest upbringing, he achieved much in business through fierce determination and hard work.

A civil engineer, his tuition was paid by money his mother saved up selling cream and eggs from their farm in Southern Saskatchewan.

A Seamstress, a Hatmaker, a Radio Fixer

Long before finishing high school, he was fixing radios. He learned his trade well and headed for New York city and haunted recording studios and radio stations. Soon he was experimenting with yet to be perfected forty-five rpm singles and twelve-inch LPs. Blessed with superb long-term memory, he had many interesting stories to tell, collected throughout his colourful life.

He worked as a naturalist in his early life then took up bird carving. He captured the attitude and stature of each of the birds he carved. He played the guitar and sang in bands, in bars, and around the campfire.

Worked in the auto parts industry and enjoyed learning how machines work by taking them apart and reassembling them.

A consummate businessman, he endeavoured to pass on his lessons in thrift and business opportunity, carefully learned during the Great Depression, to his children and grandchildren.

She was a skilled seamstress, tailor, hatmaker, and expert bridge player.

She will be missed by her loyal customers at the hair salon.

During high school, he earned money first by milking cows on a local farm, then doing custodial work and developing a business selling vacuum cleaners door to door. He was an entrepreneur at heart, a skill put to use in every aspect of his life.

Union Members

A fifty-year member of the International Brotherhood of Electrical Workers (IBEW) Union.

A union leader, he organized certification drives and labour actions. He was a husband—a few times. His heart stopped during surgery.

A life member of the Canadian Union of Postal Workers.

A member of the International Union of Operating Engineers.

Passion for Flying, Nursing, Business, and Bugs

She loved bugs and studied entomology, then worked at Agriculture Canada's entomology lab.

b.1928. A meticulous and trailblazing businesswoman. Despite having been orphaned at a young age, once set free, she was unstoppable. Loved for her sincerity and befriended by many who later became her travel companions. Visited fifty-nine countries. Uncompromising, strong and a true patriarch (although a woman).

Nursing was her first career and the operating room her first love.

His passion was selling life insurance.

A dedicated dentist, he was enthusiastic about his practice.

She loved her career with the Government of Canada and was proud of her professional accomplishments.

Her childhood was full of love, but it was challenged by the untimely deaths of her father when she was seven and her mother when she was sixteen. Thanks to the encouragement of the family doctor and her own determination, she fulfilled her dream of becoming a nurse. She met her husband in the operating room. She thought he was there to change a light bulb. He was a student working at the hospital to make ends meet.

He pitched his baseball team to the Eastern Ontario championship in 1939. He had a distinguished career in the federal public service, where he achieved the rank of managing director.

He enjoyed his career with the fire department and Sunday mornings with the "boys."

She loved archaeology and went on many expeditions with her husband to Syria. She was proud of her work and was published in her field of study.

Proud member of Victorian Order of Nurses. She followed her husband to the shore of Lake Superior and quickly fell in love with the beauty and splendour of that Great Lake and the people who lived there. She loved to watch the trees bend in the breeze, observe the changing of the seasons, and listen to the loons.

She proudly worked at the Yellow Pages for twenty years. Well known for her passion for accessorizing everything.

As a young man he decided to "go west" and work as a tree planter. He had a special connection with the outdoors and was a noted hunting guide.

A master tradesman in sheet metal. An unwavering zest for life.

They enjoyed diplomatic postings in Washington and England, where they entertained lavishly.

A pioneer of helicopter operations with a passion for flying. In retirement, he volunteered on Project North Star at the National Aviation Museum.

Proud of her work accomplishments, an executive assistant to deputy ministers. She travelled to the four corners of the globe, including circling Mount Everest at eighty-three in a Pilatus Porter and trekking in the Kalahari at eighty-six.

Born in England, he came to Canada as a young boy with his recently widowed mother and three younger siblings. As the eldest child, he took on much of the burden of supporting the family during the Depression. A lover of ballroom dancing and a natural born salesperson.

He prided himself on being the contractor who would do a high-quality job—right on time and on budget, taking pleasure in getting to know his clients personally. He was such a hard worker there was little down-time, just a couple of weeks vacation each year at the cottage.

He loved accounting and archives.

Jacks and Jills of All Trades

A provincial legislative guard, a Pinkerton detective and patrol officer, a paramedic, firefighter, and hospital guard.

A farm girl, a university graduate and elementary school teacher, a justice of the peace, and a police commissioner.

He worked in many fields over the years, from driving a taxi, to being a registered beekeeper, to construction, to facilities management, to a career in the federal government in records management. Trained in bodybuilding and was proud of winning first place in a Masters competition.

For over 102 years, he lived life to the full and did it his way. Farmer, soldier, chef, manager, missionary, and pastor.

A flight attendant for sixteen years, she then went to law school and worked on aviation policy and security.

A financial consultant, a bus driver, and a driving instructor.

After a long career in records management, she founded her own jewellery business and was a fixture at flea markets for many years.

After retirement, she became a school bus driver, then she moved on to become a school bus driver trainer.

The One Job in Your Life

She worked nearly forty years on the factory floor and taught her children honesty and the value of hard work.

He joined the Bank of Canada at entry level and spent his entire career there, retiring as senior manager.

A long serving employee of The Beer Store.

A twenty-eight-year career as an air traffic controller. An avid biker.

An accomplished baritone with a barbershop chorus for over fifty years.

Spent his whole life as a chef.

Forty years in the heating, ventilation and air conditioning (HVAC) industry.

A proud professional finishing carpenter with his father.

A stonemason and bricklayer for over forty years. He took long walks by himself with his walker, always on the go, right until his very last day.

For over thirty years, a firefighter, captain, and fire prevention officer.

A veterinarian for fifty years. There are thousands of grateful pet owners and animals he cared for.

His golf career spanned many years and many golf courses.

He missed only one day of work in forty-three years.

Dedicated to his long civil service career.

An active lawyer at the time of his passing at eighty-five.

He was proud of his thirty-seven-year career with the Canadian National Railway.

Retired after forty-two years of dedicated service with the T. Eaton Company.

His career as an accountant spanned seventy-one years.

His entire career was spent in the fresh meat industry.

She enjoyed a successful thirty-five-year career at an insurance company.

He had a long and enjoyable career as a captain with Air Canada.

A millwright for INCO for thirty-nine years.

A Canadian Pacific Railway conductor for over thirty-seven years.

Disappeared and Disappearing Careers

He was one of the last surviving log drivers on the Gatineau River.

A secretary He delivered milk door to door A tinsmith A diploma in stenography A telegraph operator A streetcar operator

She studied nursing, following in the footsteps of her older sister.

She worked as one of the early flight attendants when being a registered nurse was a requirement.

Trained as a shorthand typist and worked until her marriage.

In Service to Others

Inducted into the horse raising hall of fame. He strongly believed in the healing, comfort, and friendship of horses.

Worked as an addictions counsellor until he retired. A long-time friend of Bill W.

A personal support worker. His respect for the dignity of everyone made him a natural at his job.

She worked as a bus attendant bringing special needs children to and from school each day.

A nurse for many years. Particularly enjoyed working at a camp for children with polio. A loving caregiver to her mother, great aunt, and other family members.

He worked in a sheltered workshop.

Work Isn't Everything

He refused to be defined by his work.

When he first came to town, he quickly found a part time job at the city's most glamorous establishment, an aging tavern.

He provided IT consulting services despite significant hearing loss. He came to terms with an alcohol dependency and found sobriety with the help of AA. He tried to view life through a positive lens, with a little ditty of a song on his lips.

He had two careers: he managed a hotel and managed his golf clubs on the golf course.

b.1945. He started working in the mines in Sudbury as a young man and quickly found out it wasn't going to work out. He always had peanut butter and toast for his dog.

The eldest in his family, he became the family breadwinner at age twelve when his father died. He credited the air cadet movement for keeping him grounded during his teen years. He died wearing his work gloves and muck boots, clearing brush in the early spring—with a smile on his face. He went out the way he wanted to, fully participating.

A grocery store clerk. Heaven has gained an angel.

At an early age, he was a hard worker, delivering newspapers before school. In the end, he just wanted to be home with the person he treasured most and he was determined to do that.

Fifty-seven years. Well known in commercial plumbing and master plumber gas fitting. A champion modified stock race car driver.

A distiller at Schenley's. He died in his one hundredth year. Grew up on the family farm during the Great Depression and attended a one-room school where he was a sponge for knowledge.

She worked as a homemaker.

A beekeeper, he kept his family and friends in honey.

A costume designer in Montreal and New York and a professional genealogist. His father owned a car dealership, but with the Great Depression, people stopped buying cars.

He was a mechanic and a fan of horse racing.

A nurse, although she should have had a career as an interior designer.

He joined the EB Eddy company, starting as a paper mill worker.

He died at thirty-two. Thank you to his last two employers.

A hard rock miner in Noranda at the Waite Amulet Mines then the Noranda Mines. Born in Poland, in 1948 he travelled across the Atlantic on the USS General S.D. Sturgis.

An ever-loving character, firm courage, expertise in bridge, and culinary talents. A grande dame, she became a lawyer at forty-nine.

She studied at a school of haute couture and made hundreds of dance costumes for her grandchildren. Loved ballroom dancing—cha cha, rumba, and tango.

He lost his father at the age of nineteen. Their close relationship had an impact on his life and might very well have been the determining factor in the career path that he chose. He went on to work at a golf club.

Endless Variety

Bar manager She worked at the Royal Canadian Mint A mink farmer A bellhop at Yellowstone National Park He worked in the gold mines in Kirkland Lake A salesclerk in a shoe store A licenced auto mechanic She was a barber A legal translator An engraver with the British American Bank Note company A bus driver A piano player on cruise ships A chambermaid at a CPR resort hotel A race driver, always in the fast lane An electrician Remembered as one of the toughest hockey instructors

Work Ethic

She believed that Sunday was a day of rest.

A gentleman who dressed to the nines: suit and tie every work day with an impeccable work ethic.

He worked hard—maybe too hard—but celebrated life well too.

He believed success came from hard work and strong family values.

She held many jobs and was a self-proclaimed workaholic.

He was a driven, relentless worker and loyal employee for thirty-nine years.

Chapter 8

Wars, Military, Police

My generation is on the way out.
—Dr. Oliver Sacks

Memories Are Alive

And transform the past, influence the present, direct our future. Episodic memories recollecting a specific event can hold strong power over how we perceive ourselves.

For those who lived through ongoing physical or mental illnesses, their families recall and mark the memories of these experiences in obits. For those who experienced war, the overriding core of valour, bravery, sadness, loss, and despair seep into and through their obits.

Extracts from obituaries of veterans of the Second World War honour the longest living of those men and women who were part of the war's effort. They represent some of the last obits ever published from this war.

Women in Covert Operations

A switchboard operator for MI6 in London during WW2, she died two weeks short of her ninety-second birthday. She joined the navy as a WREN (Women's Royal Naval Service) and served during the war as one of fifty Canadian and American telegraphists intercepting high speed encrypted Japanese radio messages in Morse code. Later, she worked with her husband on various enterprises, from running a hovercraft operation at Expo 67 to establishing a house boating business in the Virgin Islands. She loved entertaining on a grand scale. Her hospitality and generosity were legendary.

A "Bletchley girl" during the war who cracked codes to defeat the Nazis, she worked on the Enigma machine for submarines.

During WW2, she performed valuable service of a confidential nature with British security and at Special Training School Camp X, 103, which trained covert agents for clandestine operations.

Working in signals using semaphore to message the convoys in Halifax, she joined the navy as a WREN and contributed to the war effort.

She valiantly fought with the Zoska Battalion (Poland) as an intelligence member during WW2. She fought under the code name Kropka, helping to lead to the Warsaw Uprising. Before the end of the war, she was taken captive by the Soviets and survived four years in Stalin's Siberian gulag labour camps. After being freed, she pursued her love of literature, attaining a master's degree in European literature before joining the Polish Academy of Sciences. She later moved to Canada to be with her son and family.

A WREN in the Women's Royal Canadian Naval Service during WW2, she was awarded the Bletchley Park Commemorative Badge for her work in signals intelligence.

She served in the air force as a Morse code operator during WW2, then dedicated forty years to the Girl Guides.

She worked for the Canadian Navy receiving coded messages from the convoy fleet—an important contribution to the war effort.

Worked as a cypher clerk during WW2, she grew up in a farmhouse, which became Green Gables in Cavendish PEI.

Ninety-eight years. For her war effort, she worked on an Enigma type machine at Bletchley Park. A volunteer with the Canadian National Institute for the Blind (CNIB), a bibliophile, her family delighted in choosing new books to capture her imagination.

Sergeant Major, Signaller, Plotting Officer, Nursing Sister...

The last survivor of her nursing group, one of the last WW2 veterans, and the last of her generation in both families. She joined the army as a nursing sister with the rank of lieutenant. During her army service, she met her future husband. Manhattans at the Sylvia Hotel in Vancouver and the Chateau Laurier, the opera Madame Butterfly, chocolates, 1812 Overture, anything on sale, birds, orchids, red meat, family gatherings... these were a few of her favourite things. To her children, she emphasized discipline and delayed gratification. In her own life, she loved throwing out that rule book. Indomitable, intrepid, frustrating, and loveable, she did it her way.

She slipped those surly bonds without the ceremony due a former Women's Auxiliary Air Force (WAAF) leading aircraft woman and WW2 veteran. Only I got to call her mum. She was proud of her Scottish heritage. She wore a sari while accepting an award on International Women's Day.

Raised with her brother by her widowed father. Together with her husband, she joined the air force during WW2. On his death, she faced this hardest challenge with quiet bravery and sweet independence. She forged a life of her own with love and help from fellow parishioners. As quietly and gently as she lived, she died.

A British scholarship girl at her grammar school, she then saw wartime service as a sergeant in the Women's Auxiliary Air Force with the Royal Air Force (RAF) Fighter Command and with Bomber Command 460. She was characterized by moral certainty, an emphasis on duty, and the importance of heeding one's conscience. She loved the Queen and highly valued the traditional roles of marriage and motherhood. She upheld the primacy of the Book of Common Prayer. Warm, generous, and sincere.

As a teenager, she joined the St John's Ambulance Volunteer Overseas Brigade in England and assisted wounded servicemen. Over the years, she lost friends and patients. Her final patient was her husband, and managing his passing at home was her greatest achievement.

I have written this about my life. I was proud to earn my commission in the Canadian Women's Army Corps and serve in the militia with the Royal Rifles of Canada. The greatest moments of my life all have been as a mother to the two most wonderful daughters. I've had a wonderful, blessed life.

A visual signaller for the Canadian Navy, she maintained lifelong friendships with other WRENS and was an early adopter of healthy eating.

b.1918. During WW2, she joined the Royal Canadian Army Medical Corps. Her Prairie childhood formed her love of nature, curling, and figure skating, and she battled the polio epidemic at the hospital where she worked. For forty years, she was a champion bowler.

She supported the war efforts as a stenographer for officials of the Royal Canadian Navy. She lost her brother in the war. Left high school before graduation to get a job because of necessity.

She served with the Women's Royal Naval Service during WW2 as a plotting officer. Until recently, still driving and getting the occasional speeding ticket, she was Grandma Tractor because of her insistence on cutting the lawn herself on her big red tractor until the age of ninety-four. Even then, her dry sense of humour still shocked and awed. She cooked gallons of marmalade and fussed over acres of flowers, raspberries, and vegetables.

Her early sense of adventure was quenched by serving as a WREN in the Women's Royal Canadian Naval Service during WW2.

She proudly served with the Royal Canadian Air Force (RCAF) during the war and was a staunch supporter of the CBC and loved all things Canadian.

Her mother died when she was three, and she was brought up by her grandmother. As a teen, she was a volunteer at a plastic surgery hospital and took wounded airmen for walks in their wheelchairs as well as going to dances with them. She served in the Signal Corps of the Women's Royal Navy Service. Later, she was happiest at "her station" in her kitchen where she baked and presided over her well-fed family and friends. A lively celebration of her life will happen this summer.

She was one of the 17,083 women who served in the women's division of the RCAF during WW2. She travelled across Canada as a member of the RCAF(WD) Precision Squad to encourage recruitment before she was deployed to England. Later, she recounted stories to her family of living through the bombing of London.

An avid naturalist, independent thinker, and volunteer, in 1943, she joined the Women's Royal Canadian Naval Service. She built her own house beside the Ottawa River.

A stenographer during the war with the RCMP intelligence branch.

A true Northern girl, hard-working, resilient, with a heart of gold. A bomb aimer in the war.

Served in the Canadian Women's Army Corp and posted in Holland.

Women Lives during War

She dodged bombs during the London Blitz. When her son was born with Down syndrome, she became a tireless advocate for children with special needs and their families. She taught us how persistence softened by compassion can change lives.

She was predeceased by her husband who was missing in action during WW2.

Born in Ukraine and despite the hardships of WW2, she finally immigrated to Canada and became an accomplished linguist.

Born in Holland and active in the Dutch resistance, she survived WW2. She would be happiest if you performed a kind act to assist someone in need.

As an ethnic Ukrainian in Poland, at fourteen she was separated from her family and taken as forced labour to Germany where she worked on a farm. When the war ended, she lived in several displaced persons camps, and in one, she met her husband. After they married, he had the opportunity to go to Canada on a ship that did not transport women. Nine months later, she and her five-month-old daughter joined him. She worked thirty-four years packing cookies. It was hard work, but she was determined to have a good life and help their families in Ukraine.

Born in Belgium, she became interested in Canada at nineteen after speaking with Canadian soldiers who liberated Brussels. In Canada, she reared beef cattle and loved all animals.

She worked in a bullet factory during WW2. Widowed at thirty-five with four children on her own, she took a secretarial course.

Youth at War

At sixteen, he made the necessary adjustments to his age credentials and went to war. At twenty-one, he was a war veteran.

At seventeen, he left home in small town Manitoba and rode the rails to Toronto where he joined the RCAF. He flew Mosquito bombers and was an instructor on Lancaster bombers. Until ninety, he drove seniors to medical appointments. He died at ninety-eight.

Ninety-two years. Joined the Navy at seventeen, served as a gunner with the defensively equipped merchant ships (DEMS). After the war, he worked as a newspaper pressman.

At eighteen, he joined the RAF as a navigator with the 148 Special Duties Squadron, a career in which he was very successful, never missing a destination or erring in expected time of arrival.

Enlisted at sixteen, he fought valiantly in the Italian campaign, most notably in the Battle of Ortona.

An air gunner with the RAF 433 bomber squadron at eighteen years old, he had a penchant for horse racing, farming, and snowmobiling. He loved to dance.

At eighteen, he joined the 434 Squadron as a flying officer and served in the Sixth Bomber Command. A prisoner of war during 1944 and 1945. Donations to the Royal Canadian Legion Poppy Fund.

At nineteen, he joined the RCAF in 1939. He often said, "You have to have a little fun in life."

Men at War

A decorated WW2 veteran, he served in the Netherlands, Belgium, Italy where he fought in the Battle of Ortona, and Germany where he took part in the liberation of Bergen-Belsen concentration camp.

Participated in the Normandy landings in June 1944 and served in France and Germany and the liberation of Holland, celebrating VE Day in Paris. In 1950, he volunteered and served in Korea and was present at the famed battle of Kapyong.

One hundred years. Son of a locomotive engineer, he served with the Irish Regiment in Italy. An accomplished artist, sailor, opera lover.

As he loved all things aerial, he joined the RAF. He was a bomber aimer because of his good math skills. He composed crossword puzzles and was considered a wiz at math.

In 1943, he was called to give up his dreams of becoming a doctor to join the air force. He felt his life was charmed with miracles during the war. A pilot by twenty-two, he flew the Spitfire and Hurricane with the RAF. Stories of near misses have always been thought provoking for his family. Later, he was the manager of an infamous tavern, which he ran with a style that was considered unique by the many people who called the place their second home.

He provided parachute training during WW2 and soldiered on for ninety-two years.

He has crossed the bar. He spent most of his time during WW2 at sea. Then came the Korean conflict and once again he found himself shipping out. After that, he stayed on the sidelines for about ten minutes before he took a position with the Corps of Commissionaires.

Like the telephone, he was born in Brantford, Ontario. He was a radio officer for the British Merchant Navy during WW2. During his years at sea, he travelled the world, fell in love with the woman who became his wife, and saw action in every major theatre of the war. He fought in the Battle of the North Atlantic and survived numerous wrecks and torpedo attacks. He rarely talked about the war, telling his children that his medals were for making excellent jam. At home and for Christmases, he supplied all the tape and post-it notes. He loved to debate loudly with any who were brave enough to take him on. He had opinions on most things and was right more often than not. An accomplished public speaker and voracious reader. His basement was a labyrinth of ham radio equipment, various electronics, and half-built computers, alongside literal ham in the "food museum." A force of nature, he lived an eventful ninety-seven years before passing away almost three years to the day after the death of his wife.

He fought in the battle of Monte Cassino, Italy, and came to Canada in 1947, where he worked as a logger, a tugboat operator, and on a farm, eventually buying the farm he had worked on.

He served with the RCAF during WW2. He also worked as a tomato inspector in Prince Edward County, followed by training as a veterinarian, and he became a government specialist in artificial insemination and reproductive technologies for cattle.

A nose-gunner during WW2, he later served as a UN peacekeeper during the Indo-Pakistan conflict. His interests were telling jokes and travelling and golfing.

He was the third child in a large family of Slovak immigrants. He served with the Canadian Air Force in WW2 as an air frame mechanic. From his example, his four sons learned home construction, auto mechanics, and colourful language.

An air gunner and navigator in the air force, he loved to entertain family and friends with obscure facts and Shakespearean soliloquies.

He served with the Forty-Eighth Highlanders of Canada during the Italian and Northwest Europe campaigns, including the liberation of Holland. He took his vows as a monk and lived in a monastery but left after a number of years and entered another stage as a monk in the world.

He joined the RCAF and served as bomb aimer on a Lancaster bomber crew stationed in England. He saw action dropping food to the Dutch in Germany occupied Holland.

He was proud to have had the honour of wearing the uniform of the Royal Canadian Navy. Always ready with a song, a quote from Churchill or JFK, or his own self-deprecating humour, he was a man among men.

He fought as a gunner and bowman on landing craft during several invasions, including D-Day, where his craft was the only one among the flotilla not to be destroyed before landing.

Born in Poland in 1919, just one year after its rebirth as a free nation. He served in the Polish Forces in France and England and unable to return to communist-controlled Poland after the end of the war, he immigrated to Canada.

His theatres of service included Holland in WW2, then Korea and the Gaza Strip.

A combat cameraman, he volunteered for the Navy at the outbreak of war in September 1939 and served on Canadian warships. He was on a landing craft for the D-Day invasions at Juno Beach and for D-Day+3 at Omaha Beach. He was in London during the V-1 rocket attacks and aboard the Haida during the engagement, in which the HMCS Athabaskan was sunk. An interest in old clocks developed into a collection, and he was a member of the National Association of Watch and Clock Collectors. A lover of gadgets.

He played a role in the liberation of France, Belgium, and Netherlands and participated in the final push into Germany. Later, he worked at a mill for forty-five years.

After working in the navy in WW2, he was a school custodian. He and his wife held hands whenever they were together.

Born in Hungary, he was stationed at Dresden and survived the British/American bombing attack on Ash Wednesday, February 14, 1945, where an estimated twenty-five thousand people were killed. After the Russian invasion of Hungary in 1956, he and his wife tried to leave, failing once, then later successfully crossing the border to Austria. From there, they went on to England, where they boarded the RMS Saxonia, crossing the Atlantic to Pier 21 in Halifax. He worked at the National Research Council and was one of the founding fathers of contemporary fire safety engineering. Over his career, he authored over 100 fire science-related publications, several books, and numerous patents. He was multilingual and self-educated in numerous fields, including history, science, politics, and philosophy. In 1964, he acquired his doctorate in engineering from Vienna University of Technology, defending his thesis in German.

He took part in the liberation of Holland and worked as a peacekeeper in Vietnam. He ran his first marathon at age sixty-five.

One of six brothers in the Canadian Armed Forces during WW2, his life was brushed with good fortune. In retirement, he opened an antique doll and toy museum.

He fought in the Battle of Normandy, and he was a member of the Twenty-First Armoured Regiment. He had an unparalleled thirst for knowledge, never missing the evening news, Question Period, or his daily crossword puzzle.

An RCAF veteran, during WW2 he worked as a wireless air gunner. After the war, he apprenticed as a watchmaker to his father. His life was vibrant and colourful.

After serving as a tail gunner in the RCAF during the war, he spent his career working at Noranda Mines.

He flew in Lancasters during the war and died at ninety-three of no particular illness.

Prisoners of War

He served in the British Second Armoured Division in Greece and North Africa, captured in Tobruk and was a POW for three years.

He flew on six sorties and was shot down over Germany. He belonged to a social group of former prisoners of war.

A veteran of the Polish Army, he was taken to a Russian prisoner of war camp in 1939 and released in 1941.

At eighteen, he joined the RCAF and went overseas as a tail gunner in a Halifax Bomber. His plane was shot down over France, and he had to bail out, becoming a member of the Caterpillar Club, an informal association of people who have successfully parachuted out of a disabled aircraft. Subsequently captured, he was a POW until May 1945.

Under Attack, Wounded

He made several harrowing convoy escorts on board the HMCS St. Stephens in the Battle of the Atlantic during WW2. Well known in his small community, he often stopped on the sidewalk to chat with neighbours. He always had a bag of treats for his canine friends.

Remembered in the RCAF for having landed a CF-101B Voodoo upside down and walking away from it.

A survivor of the Warsaw Uprising, he had a traffic-stopping garden, and he filled his house with his piano renditions of old standards like Boogie Woogie, La Cumparsita, and other tangos and waltzes. A lover of all creatures great and small—from the two legged to the four legged to the webbed, furred and feathered.

He proudly served in the Royal Navy. His ship, the RMS Lady Hawkins was torpedoed and he spent five days at sea before being rescued.

He saw action as a captain with Number One Field Regiment in the campaign for the liberation of Italy. Although seriously wounded in combat, he was blessed with full recovery.

He joined the Toronto Scottish Regiment in 1939. Wounded in 1945.

He joined the Canadian army with his brother in 1939. His experiences in WW2 remained with him forever. He served in France, Belgium, Holland, and Germany where he was wounded by a landmine and suffered a concussion, broken collarbone, and shattered leg in 1945. When asked if he would like to go on a cruise, he always replied that his two crossings of the Atlantic on cruise ships modified as troop carriers were quite enough for one lifetime.

He enlisted with the Canadian army and was wounded at the Twente canal during the liberation of Holland.

A driven, passionate, private, and acerbically witty man, he came from humble beginnings in Winnipeg, an adopted boy raised mainly by his father. He was a man of serious convictions and principles—still, he lived most days enjoying a good chuckle with companions and family. He went to war as an underage soldier in 1941. During the war he went through terrible experiences—like all war veterans. He was injured by an exploding shell in Normandy and suffered the consequences of that shrapnel for the rest of his life. He did not do anything in moderation.

In Love and War

One of seven children from a very poor family in Aberdeen, Scotland. To help support the family she started working at twelve. She came to Canada in 1945 as a seventeen-year-old war bride having married a Barnardo boy who had been sent to Canada as a fourteen-year-old to work on farms. He had returned to Britain during WW2 with the 404 squadron of the RCAF. She worked at Eaton's making sixteen dollars per week, then assembly line jobs until finally managing a restaurant in a department store. Scottish through and through, she was independent until the end. We thought she would live to one hundred. She could walk farther and faster than most of us, even wearing her little clickity heels. At a recent wedding, she out-danced everyone. She loved to make the occasional trip to Casino Niagara.

She lived through the Depression and during WW2 was a member of the British Army's Artillery Unit in London during the Blitz. Later, she came to Canada as one of over forty-five thousand war brides.

He married a woman he met as a Canadian soldier during the liberation of the Netherlands. She became a war bride.

Born in County Cork, she was a war veteran who rejected the term war bride. "I didn't marry the war."

She survived childhood polio, the Great Depression, and WW2, during which time she served in the Women's Land Army working to feed Britain and had harrowing stories of living through the Blitz. Early in the war years, she met her husband. Still, she was her own woman, and on a few occasions over their sixty-three-year marriage, she reminded him that her married name was only a borrowed one.

A war bride from Belgium, she became a teacher and volunteered in classrooms into her early nineties.

She taught in London during WW2 until the school was evacuated to Kent to escape the bombing, but they soon found themselves in the direct path of the new V1 rockets heading from Normandy to London. Teaching duties now included spending nights on a roof watching the skies for buzz bombs. She joined the ranks of the thousands of war brides who immigrated to Canada crossing the North Atlantic on a converted troop ship in November 1946 accompanied by one trunk and a baby in a basket. In keeping with her democratic beliefs, she supported equal opportunity for all.

A war bride, she married a Canadian soldier and tried snowshoeing in her eighties. A member of the Canadian War Brides Association.

Children's Lives During War

At thirteen, she and her siblings and mother were taken from Poland by cattle train to a labour camp in Northern Russia at the onset of WW2. After two years, they were displaced people travelling through refugee camps in Kazakhstan, Iran, India, Uganda, and Kenya. It was difficult for her to recover from the trauma of war, but there were times of grace and happiness. As a widow, she was protected and supported by her three children.

He was the sole survivor of his entire family who perished in the Holocaust. Through persistence and a wonderful outlook, he built a successful life.

Her father died young, and her mother was killed during the Nazi occupation. She was taken from Russia to Germany.

She was not quite five at the onset of WW2. Her father was Lutheran, her mother Jewish. Determined to save his wife and little girls, her dad hid them in the countryside for the duration of the war. Constantly on the run, they avoided the terrible fate of so many Holocaust victims such as her grandmother and her five siblings. In 1951, her family immigrated to Canada where they were able to rebuild their lives. She kept apprised of current and world affairs.

Her father was an officer in the Polish Army, and her mother was one of the first women in Poland to become a lawyer. During WW2, she and her mother fled Poland to Sweden. Later, she married a fellow Polish exile.

Born in Warsaw, she attended school in difficult circumstances during the war. She joined the clandestine Girl Guides and after the fall of the Warsaw Ghetto in which she was a messenger, she spent the rest of the war in German POW camps. Later, she was awarded the Medal of Resistance and the Warsaw Uprising Cross for her valiant efforts.

Born in a small town in England, her mother died when she was twelve. At sixteen, WW2 broke out, and she was counted on to care for her younger siblings.

b.1934. As a young boy, he spent the war years on the family croft in the Scottish Highlands. Had an enduring love of long Victorian novels.

At the outset of WW2, he and his brother were evacuated to the British countryside and stayed with a kind family in Lincolnshire. Following his dream of pursuing a career at sea, he apprenticed on board merchant navy vessels, oil tankers, and cargo ships and with the Canadian Hydrographic Service, charting the waters of Newfoundland and Labrador coasts and the Great Lakes.

Born in Indonesia, she and her mother and sisters were evacuated to Australia as refugees during WW2. She became a proud Canadian and happiest on Canadian soil. Her proudest achievements included earning a BA in Greek and Latin with highest honours in 1999. She enjoyed palliative care volunteering.

As a young child, he stayed in a tent home in the countryside sheltered from London bombings.

Her father worked in an ammunition factory during the war and died during an explosion in the factory. Her mother took in boarders to make ends meet. Our mum became a widow after seventeen years of marriage, a single mother of two teenagers.

She arrived in Montreal as a child evacuee.

Families Living through War

Growing up in Poland, his childhood years were spent in an affluent, loving family. WW2 forced him, at nine years old, and his family to flee their country. They travelled through several other countries surviving dangers until they ended up in Britain. In 1954, he immigrated to Canada, gave it his energy and talents, and in turn, Canada gave him a good, happy life.

Born in Liverpool in 1922. In his life, he suffered from privation during the Great Depression and a return to war in 1939. In 1926, his family broke apart, and he was brought up in an orphanage. One sister went to a village in Wales, then became a cloistered nun. Another sister was brought up in Liverpool. His older brother came to Canada, then another brother. His mother and her children were not reunited until 1967. Ten years ago, another brother, about whom until then he knew nothing, contacted the family. Like the rest of his generation, he never complained about how hard life had been.

She grew up in Depression-era small town Alberta and saw her father and brother off to WW2.

Born in 1922 on a prosperous farm in interwar Poland thirty kilometres from the city of Lwow. The entire family was deported in freight cars to a lumber labour camp in the Altai mountains of Siberia in 1940, with one brother perishing in transit. Here, uniquely, he developed a lifelong love of the real Russian people and the Russian language. Following Stalin's amnesty in 1942, he made his way overland through Central Asia, India, and Iran, and then to several refugee camps in British East Africa, where he met his wife, Halina, also from Poland. Sill in Uganda after the war ended, they moved to Ottawa in 1949. In 2010, he applied for a Polish passport and travelled to Poland to visit his niece. Together, they visited the family farm, which is now Ukrainian territory. He extolled the rapid progress of the new Poland and extended his stay twice, even voting in that year's presidential elections. He lived with his son in the house he had bought in 1962 until just two weeks ago. He knew that he had much to be grateful for in his long life.

Captivity

She was born to Dutch parents on a tea plantation in Sumatra, Indonesia. She and her family were captured by the Japanese and spent nearly four years in a concentration camp in the jungle in Sumatra.

She was snatched from school in Poland by the Nazis to work in one of their child labour camps. After the war she worked at whatever was available.

Born in Crimea, she was working as a telegraph operator when Germany invaded the Crimean Peninsula. At eighteen, she was sent by cattle car with thousands of fellow Slavs to Germany to work in a forced labour camp. She survived the war and made her way to Canada as a displaced person in 1948, a ten-day crossing over the Atlantic on a cargo ship. She came with only the clothes she was wearing. In Montreal, she worked as a domestic and was a force to be reckoned with, unafraid to stand on principle. A woman who had seen the worst of life but chose to focus on the good.

Born in Poland and survived three years in a German labour farm. As part of the post war refugee program, she arrived in Canada in 1947. She was happiest tending her flower beds and baking.

Her father died young, and her mother was killed during the Nazi occupation. She was taken from Russia to Germany.

Great Escapes

She grew up in the midst of the Soviet occupation of Estonia and the Nazi invasion. She fled across the Baltic with her parents in 1944 and survived a harrowing overnight journey by ship across stormy, U-boat infested waters to Sweden.

Born in Austria in 1927, she walked 125 kilometres through the mountains to escape the Red Army in 1945. She survived the heartbreaking loss of her fourteen-year-old daughter.

He escaped the Nazi occupation of Austria, later becoming an art historian and polyglot.

1934. Born in Rangoon, Burma, her family escaped to Bombay in 1942 during the Japanese invasion.

Her happy childhood in Holland ended with the war and the invasion of Holland. With good luck and the kindness of strangers, she and her family made their way to Switzerland. She had a long career in Jewish education.

Born in Krakow, Poland, he fought in the Polish Underground Army during WW2 and escaped to Sweden in 1947.

She lived in Poland under terrors and privations from both Soviet Russian and Nazi Germany occupations. She lost her home twice in bombings and lost her sister and other family members. When she fled from the advancing Soviet Front in 1944, she realized she couldn't go home again and finally reached Austria, then arrived in Canada in 1948. She regarded being well-dressed as the ultimate act of defiance in the face of adversity.

A Holocaust survivor, he was on the first Canadian War Orphans Project ship to enter Canada in 1947. He was taken in by a family in Montreal and thrived in Canada.

After Effects of War

Born in Prussia, the family fled from the Russian Army during WW2. He apprenticed as a blacksmith and immigrated to Canada, one of a few countries that didn't have compulsory conscription into the military.

Born in Latvia, she fled Europe during WW2. She could sew up a storm: doll outfits, ballet costumes, stuffed toys in need of repair, extra pockets for purses. We hovered in the kitchen like starved seagulls, waiting to pounce on her food. She laughed out loud at TV sitcoms and always gave me the gin-soaked olive from her martini. Every summer our annual long car trip to Florida was sort of like a hostage drama but with breaks for sightseeing.

She married an RCAF officer in 1943, then saved every penny so that when he returned in 1945, she was able to put a down payment on the house in which they raised five kids and lived in for seventy-three years.

She survived two global pandemics, two world wars, and the Great Depression. She came of age with a stock of strong women.

She met her husband at a YMCA dance, and they corresponded during the war until he was injured on D-Day. He returned home and they married.

Her mother and her ten siblings lived through the Depression and the Nazi occupation in Holland. After the war, she and her sister worked as nannies in London to improve their English skills. In Canada, they saved money to sponsor the rest of their family.

He survived both the Holocaust and the Hungarian Revolution.

Throughout her life, she never forgot the sacrifices made by the mostly young men from her high school, and she taught her family to be thankful for the freedom won by the sons of families in the valley.

She lived through the Great Depression and the war years, both of which shaped her view of humanity in a positive sense. She remained frugal yet generous and understood the difference between want and need in a way that people from that era can appreciate. Her views were decidedly left of centre and she embraced the changing demographic of her neighbourhood with openness and optimism. Lived independently in her home until the very end at the age of ninety-three.

Born in Romania where she lived through WW2 and the subsequent communist regime. Later, as a psychiatrist she worked extensively with Holocaust survivors. A small woman with big energy.

On the occasion of their wedding, his fellow RCAF officers provided them with a Military honour guard, a cherished gift.

A survivor of the hardships of WW2 and later a participant in the 1956 Hungarian Revolution, he immigrated after a lengthy stay in several Austrian refugee camps. With a Hungarian-English dictionary, he took whatever jobs he could.

A war-time baby born in Poland, the war and post-war years in Germany were difficult for the family, leading them to immigrate to Canada. Although not a particularly good student, he persevered.

Born into a world of war, she knew loss as a child.

What we call the beginning is often the end,
and to make an end is to make a beginning.
—T.S. Eliot

Remembering and Speaking

A proud WW2 veteran and retired firefighter who enjoyed simple things—the beauty of a sunset, a double double, his morning newspaper.

Her brother's plane crashed in WW2 and was not found until nineteen years later.

A WW2 radar specialist, he passed away six months after his wife. He said, "Life was not always easy, but it has been fun. You just have to jump in and try!"

He proudly wore his uniform every Remembrance Day..

He asks us to recognize that a daily act of kindness is always appreciated.

Her father died in a bombing in London.

The last surviving brother of four WW2 veterans.

Other Wars, Revolutions, and Resistance Movements

b.1935. A freedom fighter during the Hungarian Revolution, he enjoyed ballroom dancing and picking mushrooms. A passionate fan of boxing, wrestling, and car racing.

On May 13, 1969, major riots took place in Kuala Lumpur. She was a teacher in Malaysia and of Chinese descent and witnessed atrocities against Chinese people. Later, she taught school in the Northwest Territories.

Born in Prague, he was actively involved in the Czech resistance against the communist party and endured time as a political prisoner. In 1968, he led his family of four in a dramatic night time escape to Vienna.

b.1941. Born in Hungary, following years of suffering through the post war years of fascism and communism, he escaped with his three older brothers, travelling through Europe to England and finally on to Canada. After working in a silver mine in the Yukon, followed by many other jobs across Canada, he moved to Saskatchewan to finish high school, then on to university to get a degree in economics.

A Korean war veteran, fluent in five languages and a music connoisseur, she will be remembered for her Nanaimo bars.

In 1957, he fled communism in Hungary. Five years later, he received his citizenship and lived as a proud Canadian. His short stature was ideal for wrestling, and he earned many honours in his youth. Played banjo and harmonica.

A member of the Royal Canadian Navy, he served in a battleship, an aircraft carrier, two cruisers, although most of his sea time was in destroyers, including HMCS Sioux in the Korean War.

Following a career in the RCAF during the Korean War and a few unfulfilling positions, he decided to try his hand at teaching.

A veteran of the Korean War, he spent his last day visiting a legion hall.

Military and Police

Some people, called to certain types of service, joined to help their family or from an earnest, long-time interest, and at times a sense of excitement.

He joined the police force to protect those less fortunate and was directing traffic when his bride-to-be crossed the street.

RCMP superintendent, retired. We are sure that heaven will be more law abiding, more litter-free, and the gardens well tended now that he is there.

As an RCMP officer, at one point he guarded the prime minister. Oh, and he left a lot of stuff for a garage sale. The three sons will be taking his ashes to his hometown, and a good drink(s) will be shared in his honour.

Born on a farm in British Columbia. With an interest in military service since boyhood, he enrolled as an officer cadet in the Canadian Armed Forces. Forty years later and retired, he adopted a life afloat navigating the lakes, rivers, and canal systems of Ontario, Quebec, and Vermont.

He lost his father as a teenager and the eldest of six, he enrolled in the armed forces to support his family.

As a teenager during the Great Depression, he left the family farm, riding the rails and holding a succession of odd (sometimes very odd) jobs before enlisting in the RCMP in 1943. He treasured his three tough years stationed in Pond Inlet on the northern tip of Baffin Island where he developed a life long affection for the land. His sharp mind, incredible storytelling, irreverent sense of humour, and easy laugh stayed with us to the end. "Stop me if you've heard this one."

A self-made man, he left home at sixteen and after several years joined the air force. He finished high school by correspondence.

Married to the Force

First-class military wife and role model for her daughter.

A clerk with the RCMP, she married her husband after the war ended. At that time, RCMP policy forbid the employment of married women.

Above all, she loved being a soldier's wife.

Straightforward

He joined the RCAF at seventeen and later piloted his home-built plane. He was opinionated.

She joined the Royal Canadian Navy in 1954 as a nursing officer. For the next thirty years she was posted in units across Canada.

Born in England, he joined the British Royal Marines and travelled the world. After that, he worked as a chef in a hospital, then as a chef in one hotel, then another until he joined the Commissionaires.

Born in Labrador, she nursed with the Canadian Forces and in communities in Newfoundland and Northern Labrador.

A retired RCMP mechanic, he had fond memories of playing around the campfire alongside his brothers and sisters.

In 1962, he joined the Royal Canadian Naval Air Service and served on every ship that carried aircraft.

He participated in Arctic military manoeuvres.

At eighteen, he ventured west to train at the Royal Canadian Mounted Police Depot in Regina, then served twenty years with the force.

An active speaker for crime prevention, he coached many police officers for their promotion interviews.

A musician at heart, he served with the RCMP band then retired to a life of music, woodworking, and time with family. He instilled in his children a dedication to duty and hard work.

Purpose and Pride

b.1937. She joined the RCAF where she was honoured as the youngest flying officer in Canada and the USA at the time. She also edited and translated exquisite books of art. Although her health was ailing, she would not be denied her travels, wines, and cheeses of the world.

He had a passion for policing and the law. He spent hours telling stories about his grand adventures to all who would listen.

He witnessed the bombing of England in WW2. Later he won a spot on the RCMP Musical Ride and honed his skills in forensics. Retiring, he conquered the game of golf, became an avid cyclist and skilled furniture maker, then rediscovered his love of horseback riding and archery before finally trying his hand at painting.

Fiercely loyal, a patriot and a soldier, he lived a big life. With a supreme gift for music, he earned nationwide acclaim as pipe major sergeant with the Canadian Armed Forces band as a bagpiper.

A member of the Order of Military Merit from his days in the Royal Canadian Navy. After leaving the military, he was employed as manager of an operating room of a hospital. Survived by his beautiful bride of sixty-five years.

Chapter 9

A Great Day for Obits

And did you get what
You wanted from this life, even so?
I did.
And what did you want?
To call myself beloved, to feel myself
Beloved on the earth.
—Raymond Carver

On certain days, I open to the obituary page and realize it's a great day for obituaries. These days arrive as expansive, full-bodied obit days, with lives standing out in their complexities. Another day, a number of obits tell of people exactly my age. Some days, many people much younger.

As a small girl, uneasy and unsure of my place as the youngest in my family of four, I worried about fitting in. On our block, I ranked among the youngest of the thirteen girls and often returned home crying, upset that I was considered too small for a game, or not good enough to hold the ropes for Double Dutch, or not permitted to play bullseye marbles. Playing outside, I understood I was on the margins, still I strove to belong, as I did in my family.

As they grew up, my daughters and I were a family, all in, our commitment toward belonging, everyone feeling we were inside the fold. How else to do it.

Family members may feel that the values, commitments, and activism held by their deceased ought to be part of the story of who they were, what they stood for and dedicated their lives to. These obits, less concerned with experiences or personalities, focus on personal ethics, characteristics, and values.

Worldviews and Life Philosophies

b.1955. Like Mother Jones, he would mourn the dead but fight like hell for the living. Either Our Times or LabourStart will benefit from your support. In the words of the Big Lebowski, "The dude abides."

b.1933. Involved with Amnesty International Canada, a Quaker, a mother, and great spirit.

As a teenager and as a struggling university student he supported several children in another country through an international organization. He died at seventy-three, content with a life well lived.

He believed in fairness, ethical behaviour, and environmental stewardship. He expected nothing less than the highest quality of work, especially from himself. He loved the arts and beauty and remained respectful of those who did an honest day's work—as he called it. His most cherished memories were gained far from human settlement, often in a dog sled or a canoe.

She lived stubbornly and fought easily. She was a firearms aficionada.

She had a deeply felt social conscience and was a dedicated volunteer.

An ongoing commitment to an optimistic vision of Canada, one in which education and ideas are valued and where there is equality among all and protection of the environment.

He was committed to social justice.

A talented mason, at twenty-one his life was cut short by a momentary lapse of reason, which was a contradiction to the wisdom he attained through his pursuit of knowledge. Always respected the views of others regardless of his own beliefs.

102 years. There was, at last, a final surrender of the battlefield of life. Hitched his soul to a seagull and soared into the great hereafter. A disciplined saver and modest spender. He kept a snug lid on his emotions.

Stepping Up

An ardent supporter of the civil rights movement and a fervent anti-Vietnam war protester, she participated in many marches.

She happily baked for soup kitchens.

b.1946. Throughout his adult life, he was able to donate blood many times.

She was a tireless advocate for the disabled, disadvantaged, and marginalized. Advocated for those whose voices are not heard loudly enough by decision makers.

Seventy-four years. Born in Hungary, his parents were Holocaust survivors, his mother had been sent to Auschwitz. Their experiences imbued him with the cause of democracy and freedom. A retired postal worker and a Marxist-Leninist social and political justice advocate, he was well known in the solidarity movements for the rights of Cuba, Palestine, and Venezuela.

A strong devotion to philanthropic endeavours.

b.1947. He would give his last coins to those he felt needed them more than he. He would wish only that the spirit of giving would continue.

She was an ardent advocate for children's rights, Indigenous rights and social justice. She revelled in each experience of making new friends.

He dedicated his life to the wellbeing of others.

A strong devotion to philanthropic endeavors.

Remembered for challenging convention and for his integrity during difficult times.

She leaves a legacy of inclusiveness.

Angling for a Better World

A rebel of the sixties, he hoped for a world of truth. He was one of the sensitive ones. A visionary who strove for perfection and order and caring. His passion for literature was legendary. In the world of books, art, and history, he discovered and safeguarded the wise and hopeful and beautiful products of mankind's wisdom of mind and heart.

A committed environmentalist, she spent her career making the world a better place for all.

He was fiscally conservative and socially progressive, interested in social justice, a better health care system, and education for all. A computer pioneer. Having a good time meant travelling, hiking, running a boy scout troop, and being a pain to politicians at all levels of government. Charities: TVO, the Canadian Centre for Policy Alternatives, and the Council of Canadians.

He denounced government spending deficits and the misuse of public funds while promoting procedural fairness and natural justice.

Born in England where he registered service as a conscientious objector and worked at an accident hospital. From the age of fourteen, one of his principal interests had been jazz music, and he was recognized as an authority on the subject. By political persuasion, he was a member of the NDP.

Chapter 10

Everyone Has a Story

Others may wish family members heal through grief with celerity and firm resilience, heal as though cauterizing a wound, covering it over, a swift and strong forging forward to something and somewhere. But to grieve how life was, how it is, how to be in the world yet not quite ready, how to muster resilience, how to understand the loneliness of missing someone. How to tell that story.

Roots

One hundred years. A proud French Canadian. Her ancestors arrived in Canada with Samuel de Champlain in 1610.

Born in Rexton, New Brunswick, and brought home in a horse and buggy to Kouchibouguac. To go to school, she crossed the river in a dory.

A proud descendent of the United Empire Loyalists.

She traced her family lines back to their roots as early settlers of New France.

Born on a Manitoba farm, but it was lost during the Great Depression.

Born in a modest farmhouse in Black River, New Brunswick.

His years of genealogical research traced his family back to the 1700s in Nova Scotia.

She was born of great Prairie stock.

Her family tree in Canada extends to 1647.

In the 1930s, years of poor crops followed by drought forced her family to move east from Alberta.

Born during the Depression on a farm with no electricity, to a recent widow.

A proud Maritimer.

A first-generation Canadian.

Born in St John's Newfoundland, she immigrated to Canada with her husband in 1937.[1]

To Canada for Love, Adventure, a Better Life—or Just Because

Came to Canada and fell in love with the climate. Only later in life did he come to his senses. He fell in love with Marie, but at age nineteen in Quebec, she could not marry without her father's permission. They ran off to Ontario and eloped. He had his son watch the news at the tender age of four.

Born in 1933 in Johnstone, Scotland. His love of the beauty of his homeland, its music and dance, never left him. His love of his adopted country, Canada, began at seventeen when he visited with the Air Training Corps. In 1957, he returned.

Came to Canada in 1955 to marry his sweetheart. Like many immigrants, he worked in several occupations before establishing himself as a skilled machinist and welder.

Born in Belfast and came to Canada in 1958 to marry the cutest sailor in the fleet.

1. Newfoundland joined Canada in 1949.

Worked in retail for over twenty-five years where she made friends with colleagues and customers alike. Loved to share a laugh and the odd glass of wine or smoke.

She moved the family from "The Troubles" in Northern Ireland. She could talk the legs off a tea kettle.

In 1956 and eighteen years old, she boarded a ship off the coast of Italy, with nothing but a suitcase and her unfailing sense of hope in tow.

Immigrated from Holland in 1951 to escape the economic hardship that ensued after WW2. The family settled in Prince Edward Island. She worked at a bank, then as a manager of a grocery store. Her true love was carpentry and gardening.

Came to Canada to build a better life for his girls. Owner of a beauty salon, he worked six days a week, retirement not an option. He never failed to open his shop at 7:00 each morning until four months ago when his Alzheimer's progressed to where he could no longer work.

She immigrated to Canada from England at the age of twenty-six with her best friend Mary. She never married.

Born in Dumbarton, Scotland, she set sail for Canada in 1951 as a beautiful and courageous young immigrant leaving her parents and many siblings behind.

He came to Canada in 1951 ready to tackle a new language and cultural challenges and succeed in a new world.

Born in County Londonderry, Northern Ireland, the tenth child with eleven siblings. He made many trips back to his homeland, instilling a lifelong interest of its culture and history in his children. He managed to visit every continent at least once.

Ninety-three years. Born in a small village in the Tatra Mountains in Slovakia, she proudly retained her Slovak traditions and language. Predeceased by her son, who died tragically.

Seventy-six years. Born in Dundee. She travelled to Canada on The Scythia with her mother and sister in 1957. Although she tried to miss the boat, we're all happy she made the trip. Went to hundreds of craft shows.

Born in the Orkney Islands, she was always Orcadian. Dairy and potato faming were the education of the early days.

b.1941. Emigrated from England during Expo 67. He had to take on a large debt for which he wasn't responsible so he moved in with my family as a boarder until he could get things sorted out. We married two years later.

Seventy-five years. Born in Chkalov, Russia, and raised in Riga (then Russia), Poland, and Israel. In his fifties, he became a pedorthist and had the great pleasure of helping people manage their foot pain.

She loved to go back to Britain to visit her best friend of seventy-seven years.

A true Welshman at heart   A proud daughter of Iceland

From County Antrim, Northern Ireland   Born in eastern Slovakia

Immigrated from Norway   From San Miguel Island, Portugal   From Finland

From Ukraine   From the Netherlands   From Yorkshire   A proud Scot

No Flowers Please

We give flowers for happiness, for love, for celebration, and we give flowers as condolence—or at least we used to.

Now, no one wants them. For so long the symbol of sympathy and remembrance, flowers are now replaced by in lieu of, or flowers gratefully declined, and requests for donations to specific organizations and charities: The Sew What Club or a no-kill animal rescue. Life-affirming acts are urged: On mom's memory sing a song, dance with your sweetie, and keep the music playing.

Who follows the suggestions and donates to a small international organization, research into a rare disease, a Go Fund Me request, a youth basketball team, a local community group, a homeless shelter, or a mental health group?

In lieu of flowers, thank a random police officer for their service. Or go ahead and fix that deck, or that loose tile, or that rusty hinge you've been meaning to get to for weeks.

A registered organ donor, his generosity saved four people's lives. Consider donating your organs.

A special request from her children, donations to a women's alcohol rehabilitation centre.

Exchanged the mortal realm for the invisible realms. Remaining on the earth plane in varying stages of health, confusion and grief are his wife, sister, son, and daughter. A celebration will be held with him as the guest of honour. In the interim, please commit many random acts of kindness to the unsuspecting in memory of him.

To honour him, donate your blood.

As a nurse and in full bloom during the war years, she was an inspiration and motivation to those wounded and weary from the horrors of wars. This one-time beauty mercifully surrendered her final breath as her soul set sail on the Sea of Eternity. Having outlived her three siblings, she leaves behind her life-long love who, united for seventy-two years, may not long endure this parting. She was Every-woman: her courage of faith imbued her life, sustaining her through a debilitating bout of polio and against doctors' advice, a life-threatening pregnancy, resolute to accept whatever fate her God decreed. She had patience, raising four preschoolers at once and laughing at her husband's umpteenth telling of his humorous tales. Modest and reserved in a charming way, slightly self-critical and self conscious, but ruled by a tender heart. Instead of donations, give a mom, any mom, a big, long hug today.

Disabilities did not hold him back. We thank his friends for their kindness. We ask you to show kindness when you meet people with disabilities.

To a seniors' support organization   Stephen Lewis Foundation

To Propeller Dance   Child Haven International

The charity of your choice would be appreciated   Alcoholics Anonymous

In his memory, hug a loved one   Mothers against Drunk Driving

Since the garden was her favourite place, consider planting a perennial in your garden in her memory.

Donations to Therapeutic Paws of Canada   Donations in support of AIDS research   Right to Play

For those wishing to make a donation, please consider the Grey Sisters.

Spinal Cord Injury Canada   Aboriginal Head Start Program

Your local food bank   Canadian Nurses Foundation

Wounded Warriors   Mums stop the harm   Movember   The Canadian Association of Disabled Skiers

To a small dog rescue   UNHCR

The Canadian Mental Health Association   David Suzuki Foundation   Oxfam

Thank You To

The coroner for doing her job in a respectful manner.

The kind individuals who pulled him from the water and performed CPR on him and the police and paramedics who attended to him afterward.

The MAID programme.

His caregivers for the past twenty years who were so considerate of him since he was sixteen.

Her paramedics.

Chapter 11

Death

We're all just walking each other home.
—Ram Dass

Friend

Day one: I turn the last corner to her home at the end of a nine-hour trip. She stands on her front deck, both arms enthusiastically waving me towards her. Full of life. She can't be dying. Bandana on her head, cane in her right hand, but still. Dinner, lobster mac and cheese, which she savours joyfully, eats as much as I do as we drink celebratory bubbly wine. We laugh heartily, tell ribald stories, and chat with vigour, as always. But I'm confused, unable to believe.

My best friend, no, more than best friend, no word yet for what that is. We joke and we talked intensely but never about sorrow around dying. No allowance, no patience for an "aah," an "oh dear, that's not good"; rather, a strict "stop there" in response to me, shocked and saddened by her diagnosis. She wants nothing that circles compassion and certainly no pity. She did though want me to fly there when she knew there were four to six weeks remaining, told me that straight-forwardly, and yes, the joy in her voice when my ticket was bought. "I can't wait for you to come." Me, full of fear, of crying in front of her knowing she wouldn't want that, of seeing her shimmering skull, seeing her eyes too large, seeing her jutted bones as proof. How to smile, banter, tell tales of our wild times, times when the moment was everything. Of when we were passionate. Of the times we crossed the country to see each other again and again. Until friendship won out, for the best.

Times I cried, that much of what she said, what she thought of me, mattered. Times I angered, times she accused me of not being a faithful enough friend, and those times I did the same. Times we refused to understand a decision made, an action taken, until we somehow smoothed things over.

The best, the closest, the one who withstands the diversions, the changes, the resistances. A thought or many more each day, a phone call almost each day, anticipation for the other's voice.

The personality changes she made as she was dying: her three-year sentence with no escape. Her better self emerging more and more to a close-to, but not quite, tenderness towards many. Often times during her final week she repeated, "I live in the moment." This from her: a planner, a doer, always with a project on the go alongside a new one in her mind in the midst of assessing, reassessing, preparing to set it in motion. I live in the moment coincided with "I'll do this, my idea is solid."

Day two: She drives us in her car for ocean views, trees, hills, tight winding roads, stopping at Jessie's to pick up cod caught early that morning. A cinq à sept on her front deck, glorious sunshine, a red and white lighthouse to our right, one small motor boat in the ocean straight ahead. Wine in hand.

Day three: A drive to view art displayed in nearby towns and outports and coves. This time someone else drives. She doesn't leave the car, waits to know what the art was like, did we enjoy it? Driving home, she slumps unconscious in the passenger seat. Only for minutes, but a turn. Later that day, we attend a neighbour's afternoon garden party. Umbrella guarding her from the sun, she takes a few sips of something in a glass, accepts no snacks, says little, but listens, follows conversations. She's not her usual centre of a gathering. Tired, she needs help getting home, where she rests.

Day four, very early morning: A fever fills her body, her temperature too high, her body burns. Not exactly conscious and not quite unconscious. Liminal. Not able to walk to the car to go to the hospital an hour away. An ambulance arrives.

The small hospital cannot do much and it takes hours too long to remove her pain. More and more, she is only sort-of conscious. A smile at times, an "uu" for I hear you and a higher pitched "uu" for yes. Tired, unable to eat, although hospital staff bring fish and chips for lunch, porkchops for dinner.

Day five: Unconscious, her pain noticed, visible. With no reason to stay in the hospital and her long-stated goal to die at home, she is returned there and set in her bed with a glorious view of the North Atlantic Ocean—although she can't, anymore, see it.

This is too fast. I'm not ready. I want more time with her, but I now know I don't have it. "Live in the moment." This moment, do what's best, now, stay here, right here, in this moment, no past, no future, just the now.

What I want to say to her about the past, about the present, the future. But I don't. I sit, watch while each of her inhalations seems to arrive more slowly, requiring more effort. The hard work of the breath. It continues. At midnight, "Goodnight. Sleep well, I'll see you in the morning. I will."

Day six: 7:15 AM, her last moment of ragged breath. Her wife, her witness beside her. I go to my friend, kiss her forehead, hold her hand, stroke her arm. We all sit beside her on the bed, quiet, then talk in whispers, cry, pass a tissue box. At 10:30 AM, a funeral station wagon arrives for her drive to the crematorium. We stand on her deck as she drives by, waving to her slowly, sadly, attempting to be stalwart and brave.

It was her, several provinces away, whom I phoned in the middle of the night when my daughter died. The next day she rang my doorbell, stayed with me for a week, held me as I cried, and made tea, too much tea, made me drink it. Cooked meals, answered calls on my behalf. Held me over the stunned, the shocked hump of turning the incomprehensible to a sort of belief without understanding, no acceptance. Sheer grief.

Twenty days later: "Live in the moment." This is my moment. At my kitchen table. I drink tea from a small cup. I'm as exhausted as grief can make me. I do little, avoid friends, reply with "I'm lying low for a while," hoping that covers it. I want to stay away from the spin of the world, not ready to emerge, not prepared to be in the world without my best friend, who I relied on for being my best, my closest, who taught me many things, who once, after my daughter Alessandra's death, held me through grief.

How Death Comes

Mother and daughter, as a result of a car crash. The daughter was the new owner of an apple orchard, lavishing care and attention on the apples to produce a healthy crop of nutritious, tasty fruit. Fondly remembered by family and their playful dog. A celebration of life for both will be held at the orchard, a place they both adored.

He had an extensive history library with books from ancient Egypt to the Atomic Age. He died from Covid at sixty-three in hospital in isolation and pain.

Her first words when she woke up the morning she turned one hundred were "I made it!" She probably thought that reaching 101 would be an anti-climax, so she left this world eleven days short of her next birthday.

She was moved by the call of the loon and cherished the silence and beauty of dawn. It seemed only fitting that she left us as dawn was breaking Sunday morning.

In the early afternoon of a lovely day, she went for a swim in the lake at her cottage. After only seven or eight minutes she stopped moving. Resuscitation was unsuccessful. Autopsy found a healthy heart, the cause of her cardiac arrest unknown.

After enjoying a wonderful Christmas day at her daughter's home.

He drifted away as the sun set.

He lived life with a big heart, although sadly, that's what took him.

He developed asbestos-related lymphoma from the work he did.

Her many years of suffering have come to an end.

He lived his 102 years to the fullest. He had planned his Grey Cup party at his residence, fell short of breath, and passed away while singing. But the party with his friends went on in celebration of his spirit and how he played the game. He played fair; he made every touchdown count.

She did not die peacefully, but she lived joyously.

Tragically from a collision with a distracted driver.

Where We Take Our Leave

Our sister died unexpectedly in one of her favourite places, the library. Her love of four-legged creatures was shown by rescuing many abandoned cats.

On a much-loved fishing trip with good friends, he had just reeled in a fish. He got more done in a morning than most of us did all day.

He passed away unexpectedly from an aortic aneurism suffered while golfing with friends.

After returning home from his daily long run. In the comfort of his own home.

On his way to warmer weather.

While hiking with his wife.

While visiting family in Ireland.

Died at home with her foster sister.

Died quietly at his home. Survived by his special granddaughter and his step-grandson.

How long does a lifetime last? If one stops to consider,
it is like a single night's lodging at a wayside inn.
—Questions and Answers about Embracing the Lotus Sutra,
WND-1

When We Go

In the continuous process of becoming, we die at a particular juncture of this becoming.

At twenty-two in a one vehicle accident. He had so much potential.

She never got to realize her wish to turn one hundred, as she passed away at the age of eighty-one. Make a donation to your local food bank. This would make her smile.

At thirty-three, he got his pilot's licence and was a close friend with his two cousins. As fate would have it, the three cousins died within days of each other.

After a ninety-seven-year run, he passed away.

At the tender age of fifty.   Passed away at sixty-five and change.

After ninety-two great years.   Two weeks after her ninety-eighth birthday.

Passed away on her ninety-ninth birthday.   A few days short of ninety -three.

In her 102nd year.   103 years old.   109 and six months.   He was 107 years.

Mum passed away suddenly and with great sadness at the age of eighty-six.

On the first day of summer in her seventieth year.

The Mystery

In a family where personal stories were rarely passed on, I nonetheless believed I was similar to my Aunt Lyda. Like her, I played the piano and loved skiing. She however was killed by a car in the Laurentians while on a ski holiday with four girlfriends some time in the late 1930s.

This occurred long before I was born. Lyda, my mother's sister and eldest of seven children, was twenty-five when she died. Every two weeks, she had brought home her paycheck for the family. Her mother was already a widow and already one child had died and another shortly following Lyda's death. No further information about Lyda's life now exists and no obituary for her was kept. I will never know whether her obit may have provided a small entrance to the woman she was, the woman I might have resembled.

What an obit merely suggests, what it hides. The gap between how the deceased would have appreciated their life depicted and how life actually was for those who lived and interacted with them. The similar gap we hold between what others know of us, what we suggest, what we hide.

The stories we all have. The stories that will be told about us.

Chapter 12

Obituaries for Some Day

The Death Columns

Having lived my whole life as a newspaper obituary page, I must now report my death. Alas, I am aged but even so this feels too soon. No doubt I will be mourned by many sincere readers, yet poorly mourned by my numerous online progenies, whom I will not name. I have had a compelling, varied, and satisfying life, having supported many in the midst of their critical times and grateful that I have often been found captivating. I was proud to consider myself the best-read page as well as an important people's history. I wish to thank those who, by working tirelessly and daily, took good care of me as well as those who defended me when ill-wishers deemed me morbid and lugubrious. Although I am aware that I will be missed by many, there will be no wake or celebration of my life and no need for flowers. As Bob Dylan said, "The times they are a-changin." May I live in your memories.

Donna McCart Sharkey

She loved people, stories, and stories about people. She was an observant reader of obituaries, and at one point, she wrote about them.

Deepest appreciation to
Demeter's monthly Donors

Daughters
Tatjana Takseva
Debbie Byrd
Fiona Green
Tanya Cassidy
Vicki Noble
Myrel Chernick

Sisters
Amber Kinser
Nicole Willey

Grandmother
Tina Powell